NATIONAL GEOGRAPHIC DIRECTIONS

INTO A PARIS QUARTIER

INTO A PARIS QUARTIER

REINE MARGOT'S CHAPEL AND OTHER HAUNTS OF ST.-GERMAIN

DIANE JOHNSON

NATIONAL GEOGRAPHIC DIRECTIONS

NATIONAL GEOGRAPHIC
Washington, D.C.

Published by the National Geographic Society
1145 17th Street, N.W., Washington, D.C. 20036-4688

Text copyright © 2005 Diane Johnson
Map copyright © 2005 National Geographic Society

First printing May 2005
Paperback edition 2006, ISBN-10: 0-7922-6208-5, ISBN-13: 978-0-7922-6208-4

Photography credits: PAGES 27, 35, 93–Courtesy of the author; PAGES 6, 10, 37, 42–Monica Ekman; PAGES 71, 74, 117, 149, 192–Anne Randerson; PAGE 168–David Scherman/Getty Images

Library of Congress Cataloging-in-Publication Data:
Johnson, Diane, 1934-
    Into a Paris quartier : Reine Margot's Chapel and other haunts of St.-Germain / Diane Johnson
      p. cm. -- (National Geographic directions)
    ISBN: 0-7922-7266-8
    1. Saint-Germain-des-Prés (Paris, France : Quarter)--History. 2. Saint-Germain-des-Prés (Paris, France : Quarter)--Intellectual life. 3. Saint-Germain-des-Prés (Paris, France : Quarter)--Description and travel. 4. Paris (France)--History. 5. Paris (France)--Intellectual life. I. Title. II. Series.

DC752.S25J64 2005
944'.361--dc22

2005041514

Interior design by Melissa Farris

Printed in the U.S.A.

For John Murray, as ever

CONTENTS

INTO A PARIS QUARTIER

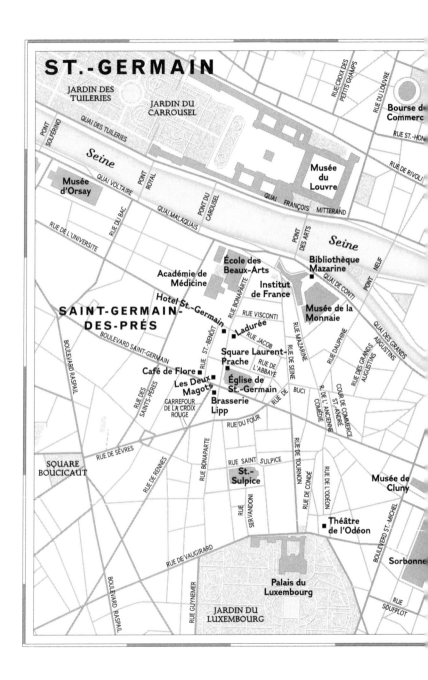

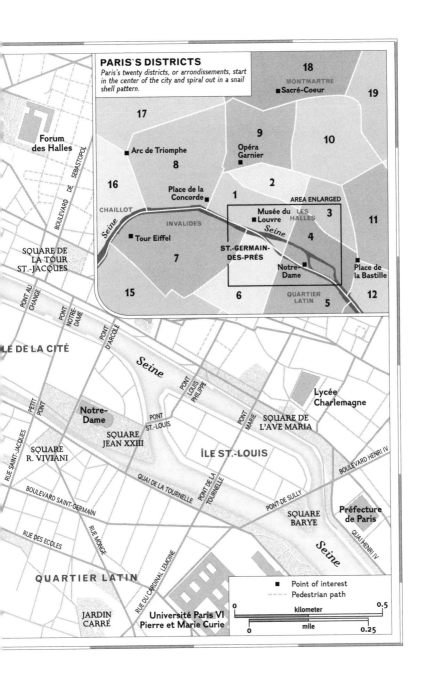

PARIS'S DISTRICTS

Paris's twenty districts, or arrondissements, start in the center of the city and spiral out in a snail shell pattern.

18
MONTMARTRE
■ Sacré-Coeur

19

17

9
Opéra
Garnier
■

10

Forum
des Halles

■ Arc de Triomphe

8

2

16

Place de la
Concorde ■

1

AREA ENLARGED

Musée du   LES
■ Louvre   HALLES

3

11

CHAILLOT

INVALIDES

Seine

4

■ Tour Eiffel

SQUARE DE
LA TOUR
ST.-JACQUES

7

ST.-GERMAIN-
DES-PRÉS

Notre-
Dame

Place de
la Bastille

15

6

QUARTIER
LATIN

5

12

Seine

LE DE LA CITÉ

Seine

PONT AU CHANGE

PONT NOTRE-DAME

PONT D'ARCOLE

PONT LOUIS PHILIPPE

Lycée
Charlemagne

PETIT PONT

Notre-
Dame

PONT
ST.-LOUIS

PONT MARIE

SQUARE DE
L'AVE MARIA

RUE SAINT-JACQUES

SQUARE
R. VIVIANI

SQUARE
JEAN XXIII

ÎLE ST.-LOUIS

BOULEVARD HENRI IV

QUAI DE LA TOURNELLE

PONT DE LA TOURNELLE

BOULEVARD SAINT-GERMAIN

PONT DE SULLY

SQUARE
BARYE

Préfecture
de Paris

RUE DES ECOLES

RUE MONGE

Seine

QUAI HENRI IV

QUARTIER LATIN

RUE DU CARDINAL LEMOINE

JARDIN
CARRÉ

Université Paris VI
Pierre et Marie Curie

■   Point of interest
- - - -   Pedestrian path

0   0.5
kilometer

0   0.25
mile

INTRODUCTION

The world's quintessential expatriate city, Paris has long held
a special fascination for Americans. Offering an incomparable
urban setting, a rich cultural legacy and a deep-rooted respect
for artistic pursuits and individual freedom, the French capi-
tal has provided a stimulating environment for successive
waves of celebrated American émigrés.

GUIDE MICHELIN, PARIS

As the traveler's bible, the *Guide Michelin,* suggests,
maybe the feeling Americans have for Paris is unlike
that of other visitors. Maybe we need it more. The
English, it seems, can take the city or leave it, full as it
is of French people: "Many an Englishman has har-
boured a secret admiration for Paris—if it were not for
the Parisians," as the editor acknowledges. The Spanish,
the Swedish are seldom seen here; these nations have
beautiful places of their own. But the City of Light has
haunted the American imagination from the days of
Benjamin Franklin and Thomas Jefferson, the reflex of

our aspirations, and, some might say, feelings of cultural inferiority or at least of newness. Paris has also occupied a significant place in our literature, from Henry James's bemused innocents to Hemingway's worldly pub-crawling expatriates.

And, like Jefferson's, like Gertrude Stein's, the American imagination has tended to fasten on a particular part of Paris: the Left Bank around the church of St.-Germain-des-Prés. Jefferson lived on Rue Bonaparte, just a few doors away on the street where I am living more than two hundred years later, and Franklin was around the corner on the Rue Jacob. The novelist Henry Miller, staying up the street in the Hotel St.-Germain—where Janet Flanner, the venerable *New Yorker* correspondent, also lived during part of her long sojourn in Paris—wrote a friend, "I love it here, I want to stay forever ... each day I will see a little more of Paris, study it, learn it as I would a book. It is worth the effort.... The streets sing, the stones talk. The houses drip history, glory, romance." I feel the same.

Paris has always been a refuge and escape for foreigners, somewhere better in some sense or another than where they were, whether politically, artistically, or psychologically; whether for the fashionable lesbians of the twenties, American drunks during Prohibition, political exiles like Milan Kundera, social exiles like

Oscar Wilde, worldly writers like Edith Wharton, down-and-out English travelers like George Orwell, Russians like Ivan Turgenev and, after 1917, Vladimir Nabokov, or African Americans like James Baldwin, Josephine Baker, or Chester Himes. For these and countless others, Paris has always represented freedom and a superior grasp of things, an exemplary set of priorities that places living before other concerns, a sea of calm except when it boils up; but even during its upheavals the stranger is curiously spared, like the publisher Sylvia Beach, or Edith Wharton's lover William Morton Fullerton, an old man staying on in Paris during the Second World War.

I recently wrote an introduction to a collection of selected short stories about Paris by American writers from Hemingway's day to today (*Americans in Paris: Great Short Stories of the City of Light,* edited by Steven Gilbar), each story testifying to this special relationship between Americans and Paris. What struck me was that many of these stories were in fact about personal defeat. In most of them, the American finds he is not able to live up to the cultural demands, the Gallic eroticism (whether experienced or merely hoped for, and possibly somewhat apocryphal), the conflicting demands of home versus foreign temptation. The Americans in almost all these stories go home, like Chad Newsome in

Henry James's *The Ambassadors,* to face real life in the States, and will think wistfully forever after about what might have been, if only they had stayed, or had learned how to stay, in Paris. We are moved to ask: What is it about Paris? And what is eluding us at home?

PART ONE

Studying the Métro map

St.-Germain-des-Prés

St.-Germain-des-Prés. This old quarter on the Left Bank is known for its beautiful church as well as for its narrow streets, antique shops, restaurants, cafés and cellars. The church, the oldest in Paris, and the abbatial palace are all that remain of the famous Benedictine abbey.
GUIDE MICHELIN

The quarter of St.-Germain-des-Prés may be the most visited and written about of all Parisian neighborhoods, and at first it seemed to me that there was little to add about these oft-trodden precincts—the coffeehouses Les Deux Magots and Café de Flore, the church of St.-Germain-des-Prés itself, the Luxembourg gardens, Brasserie Lipp ... The ghosts of Sartre and de Beauvoir and Hemingway are surely tired of being invoked, the echo of Edith Piaf faintly but audibly protesting.

All these belonged to the recent past, the heyday that comes to people's minds when you say "St.-Germain-des-Prés," the era from the forties through the sixties, famous for jazz and existentialism. In many ways, those were not easy decades. France was liberated but damaged, rancorous, and poor, yet it seems to have been a time of excessive gaiety, camaraderie, artistic achievement, erotic freedom, and political change, the haunt of so many of the talented, beautiful, or merely energetic people whose names have come to be associated with it now—Jean-Paul Sartre and Simone de Beauvoir to be sure, but also the writers Boris Vian, Albert Camus, the model Bettina, African Americans like Richard Wright.

I have a friend, a painter now in her seventies who was one of the most beautiful and energetic members of the "golden age" of St.-Germain-des-Prés (others have told me; she wouldn't say that of herself), who describes the life: You went every night not to just one but three or more fashionable night clubs, a certain regular itinerary that never changed, until tourists (mostly French) turned out to view the beautiful people at play, thereby spoiling it. No one had any money, so you drank very little, usually whiskey, but you ordered a "baby," a mere drop, all you could afford. You danced—the music was jazz, often American jazz and often played by American musicians. There were dinner shows at the Club St.-Germain, the Vieux Colombier ...

It looks in photos of young women flying through the air, their New Look skirts ballooning, swung by skinny guys, as if the dance was the jitterbug. So much smoking! It almost hurts to imagine what the air was like in the Tabou, one of the most popular and famous nightclubs. At the Café de Flore, Sartre held forth, drinking and writing. He and de Beauvoir would stay there all day, especially in cold weather, and it is said they had their own telephone line. Those two, while appearing sociable, were working seriously at their philosophical writings—establishing the prevailing philosophy, existentialism, an elaboration of what in the less reflective partygoers was just nihilism and a devil-may-care attitude. The politics was communist—this was the *gauche caviar,* as well-heeled leftists would come to be called in Mitterand's time.

It is hard now, in the glossy consumer paradise St.-Germain has become, to imagine that frenetic life, and above all the intellectual spirit then. I suppose Greenwich Village, or Berkeley, or North Beach in San Francisco during the sixties, might have been equivalents nearer to home: a time of excitement, changing mores, political dissent. In Paris, people went to the Nuages bar—"That's just where you went," says my friend Marie-Claude, "you" meaning "everyone"; but everyone could not mean all of Paris—it must have only meant the fashionable world of intellectuals and artists, welded into a kind of milieu that, looking back, seems to the outsider a milieu

The famous Café de Flore

that would never have let "one" in, rather as in all those American short stories I have mentioned.

Alas, while the glamorous people were at the Tabou, someone had to be home cooking dinner. That was me during the sixties in California, a woman with small children, completely missing the *zeitgeist,* and it would have been me—and most of us, surely, during the reign of Sartre in Paris. What would one say to Jean-Paul Sartre anyway? It's me now, frankly, still marginal, contentedly mooning around the side streets, communing with seventeenth-century Parisian architecture and buying groceries for dinner, instead of hanging out at the Café de Flore. People do hang out there, though, and also at the Café Bonaparte and Les Deux Magots, crowded with people drinking coffee or wine at any hour. They are mainly tourists, but they may have always been tourists, for above all this is the haven of the foreigner, the stranger, the escapee.

Sometimes I arrange to meet a friend at one of these cafés at the end of the day for tea or a *kir royale,* often enough to get a glimpse of this public, sociable French custom, and of these cafés where so much of politics and art got started, and now continue the very long traditions of this *quartier.* The Café de Flore and Les Deux Magots have been here since the nineteenth century.

The café life is partly a function of Paris being a "walking city." Is this the place for a diatribe about the automobile? I didn't realize until I came to Paris, and I'm convinced that most Californians (Americans in general?) don't realize, because they don't have an opportunity to enjoy, the richness of a life that allows them to walk everywhere, to learn how much more fascinating and more amusing it is to walk, stopping to stare into store windows, sitting down at a sidewalk café for a coffee, meeting someone you know by chance or by rendezvous. New Yorkers have this privilege, but do the rest of us? In most of our cities, where would you walk to? Would you be safe?

THE TIME OF THE THREE MUSKETEERS

La Place Saint-Germain-des-Prés. On a demoli
pour la former un superb portail et des batîments
conventuels du XVIIème siècle.
VIE ET HISTOIRE DU VIE ARRONDISSEMENT

Modern St.-Germain is lively and prosperous, yet it is the seventeenth century, still strangely present here, that establishes its character, and I find that to understand the way it is now, it's necessary to try to see it as it was four hundred years ago. Since I have come to live on the Rue Bonaparte, the street that lies between Les Deux Magots—Hemingway's hangout—and the church of St.-Germain-des-Prés, I find that, beside the shades of Sartre and Piaf, there is another crowd of resident ghosts who urge themselves forward for recognition through four centuries. They include the Musketeers—d'Artagnan, Aramis, Athos, and Porthos; four queens—Catherine de Médicis, Marguerite de Valois (or "de Navarre" after her marriage to Henri de Navarre, later King Henri IV),

Anne of Austria, and Marie de Médicis; the sinister Cardinals Mazarin and Richelieu; Kings Louis XIII to XVI, many Henris; and numberless other misty figures in plumed hats whose fortunes and passions were enacted among the beautiful, imposing buildings of the seventeenth century still in this neighborhood. Theirs is the spirit that prevails today, and that moves me most.

In a way, I had been prepared for them. My particular connection to this Parisian neighborhood started in childhood, thousands of miles away; I was over thirty before I ever actually saw it, but when I did, I knew it well. Not that I was one of those good little French majors that had grown up dreaming of France, not at all. I am here by accident.

It was a Francophile librarian at the Carnegie Library in my hometown of Moline, Illinois, who placed in my hands, when I was nine or ten, the works of Alexandre Dumas. I read all the ones we had, in translation of course, and that is where Paris and I start, with my childhood reading of *The Count of Monte Cristo, La Reine Margot,* and, above all, *The Three Musketeers.* Was it this early passion for Dumas that preordained that I would someday live five minutes' walk from where the real d'Artagnan lived, almost on the spot where the Musketeers fought their duels, and, above all, where the romantic queens of legend, Marguerite de Valois, then Navarre, and Anne of Austria actually trod, four centuries ago?

If only we could recapture how we read when we were children, burning with interest, with breathless excitement, unwilling to put down our book to eat or sleep. Often we can remember the actual circumstances of where we were sitting, the injunctions of our parents to come to the table, or go to bed. My memory of my childhood literary enthusiasms is still vivid. I read *The Three Musketeers* on a visit to my beloved maiden Aunt Henrietta, in Watseka, Illinois, the time I nearly died.

I had come down with polio, or at least that's what doctors now say in retrospect it probably was. I don't know where my parents had gone, or where my little brother was, and I can't remember if the doctor was called. My childless aunt had not had much experience with childhood illness so was less, rather than more, concerned than she probably ought to have been; I had never been so sick and never have been since, with a raging fever, and a headache so horrible I can almost still feel it, an unusual thing, for pain is usually impossible to remember.

So my recollection of burning with reading fervor has a certain explicable component. Literally feverish, I lay on the sofa in the Victorian parlor or in bed for days with the enthralling story of d'Artagnan, Athos (my favorite), Porthos, and Aramis. They were alive for me—the Musketeers, their leader M. de Treville, the wicked Milady, the handsome Duke of Buckingham, and the beautiful Anne of Austria, she whose reputation was saved by the frantic voyage of d'Artagnan to England to replace her missing diamond studs before her husband Louis XIII could find out that she had given them to France's enemy, Buckingham. Would she get them back in time to wear them to the ball where she had been commanded to appear in them?

Hindsight changes one's reading of Dumas. I see now that I must have been given an expurgated children's edition. In Dumas's original versions, both Anne of Austria and La Reine Margot were free with their favors, but I got none of those innuendos as a child, and was surprised when rereading these books as a grown-up to find how rather explicit they are. I had never understood, for instance, that the villainess Milady de Winter seduces d'Artagnan and takes him to bed. Rereading *The Three Musketeers,* it is bound to seem today that the seventeenth-century ideas of masculine behavior— touchy honor, always being insulted, challenging each other and dueling mindlessly, rather like the young bulls in the children's book *Ferdinand the Bull,* seem, in truth, rather silly, and we should hope that men have evolved, mostly, at least in some societies. In many other places, it seems, they are still going through their Musketeer phase. Still, who would change the swash-buckling movie versions? Even though I could not accept Gene Kelly in the role of d'Artagnan, (the earlier Douglas Fairbanks was better), Lana Turner entirely suited my view of Milady, and Van Heflin, Keenan Wynn, and Gig Young made a handsome trio of Musketeers. I would see all the films over and over. Meantime, I believe I was saved from serious complications of polio by my determination to remain conscious and finish Dumas's wonderful novel.

D'ARTAGNAN

It is about a year ago, that in making researches in the
Bibliothèque Nationale ... I by chance met with the Memoirs
of Monsieur d'Artagnan, printed by Peter the Red at
Amsterdam—as the principal works of that period, when
authors could not adhere to the truth without running the
risk of the Bastille, generally were. The title attracted my
notice; I took the Memoirs home, with the permission of the
librarian, and actually devoured them.

Alexandre Dumas, THE THREE MUSKETEERS, author's preface

How do we account for the curious thrill we feel standing
in some ancient space, in the presence of some historical
artifact, thinking of all the things that have happened
here? It is surely something about immortality, the idea
of one's self connected, by being present, to the past and
to the ongoing. It was only a few years ago, before we
came to live in this apartment on Rue Bonaparte, that
one day when I was riding the 69 Bus down the Rue du
Bac, I noticed on the building at number one, a plaque

that said: "Here stood the house where lived Charles de Batz-Chastelmore d'Artagnan, captain-lieutenant of the Musketeers of Louis XIV, killed at the siege of Maestricht in 1673, immortalized by Alexandre Dumas."

Perhaps that little plaque more than anything else brought home the realization that Dumas's immortal characters had once been living people who may have conducted their sword fights on the very spot where I was standing, in what were then the fields called Prés aux Clercs, a favorite dueling ground lying around the abbey of St.-Germain between our street and the Rue des Sts.-Pères. Of course, I knew there had been a historical d'Artagnan, but I had not until then experienced that particular sense of the reality of past events that sometimes strikes with special force. Would having known when I was a child that I was reading true history have increased my excitement and pleasure at Dumas's tale? Now it was hardly possible to feel any more pleasure and excitement than was mine to have my childhood favorite again before my eyes.

Perhaps not everyone remembers the engaging young d'Artagnan of Dumas's creation. Like the hero of a fairy tale, he sets out from his native province of Gascony for Paris, to make his fortune, with only a few possessions—his father's blessing, a powerful ointment, his sword, and a yellow horse. His naïveté and cheerful, trusting nature endear him to the fierce Musketeers as much as to us. Is it too much to say that an American may find something of ourselves in his wonderment as he confronts the big city for the first time?

We know quite a bit about the historical d'Artagnan. He was born in Bigorre, in southwestern France, became a Musketeer (an elite corps of the king's soldiers) and rose in their ranks, married a rich widow, Charlotte-Anne de Chanlecy Damas de la Claixe (or Clayette), and he himself had become rich, as a captain in the Guards. In 1659 the couple moved to the corner of Rue du Bac and the Quai Voltaire, in what was later called the Hôtel Mailly-Nesle; "hotel," meaning large private house, the word not having at all the connotation of inn or lodging we think of today. Apparently they were not entirely happy, or not happier than most couples.

Something is known of the d'Artagnan household. Charlotte-Anne brought a dowry of 60,000 livres worth of property, 24,000 livres in cash, and furniture worth another 6,000, large figures for today. Their wedding, at the Louvre, was attended by the king and Cardinal Mazarin. D'Artagnan was an important and trusted minion of Louis XIV—entrusted, for instance, with the arrest and delivery of the disgraced minister Fouquet to prison, after Fouquet had had the bad judgment to build a château more beautiful than Louis's.

An inventory of the d'Artagnan property shows them to have had two carriages—one for four people, one for two, the former lined in green velvet with four mirrors and green damask curtains, the latter upholstered in red damask. It was a time when wealth was ostentatiously displayed, and it was important to display it.

They had a servant called Fiacrine Pinou, and a big table and armoire in their kitchen on the ground floor off the court. Upstairs, an antechamber and a big room was hung with tapestries of leaves and flowers—*milles fleurs,* the prettiest ones. These hung also in the bedroom on the second—third, in the American sense—floor. In the bedroom, too, a huge bed hung with striped silk was placed behind a screen, and on the wall a mirror and a portrait of Anne of Austria, the queen who d'Artagnan served so well. There was a lovely view of the Seine. D'Artagnan himself had lace gloves, silk stockings, a bathrobe lined in green satin, two swords, one with a gold handle ...

Many buildings like the one the d'Artagnans lived in contained "apartments" from a very early time, that is, apartments in today's sense of an individual habitation consisting of a number of rooms in a larger building containing several such habitations. The d'Artagnans lived in such an apartment. It is also said this style of dwelling—with many families in one building—existed in ancient

Rome; anyway, it is still the dominant way of living in Paris. Our building on Rue Bonaparte has four families, counting us.

The French novelist Boris Vian recounts that, in 1765, one William Cole, an Englishman, took lodgings on Rue Bonaparte. His rooms were in what was then called Hôtel d'Orleans "in the Fauxborg [sic] St.-Germain," which was probably across the street from us at number thirteen, looking over the gardens of the Duc de La Rochefoucauld, descendants of the author of the famous *Maxims,* a hundred years after his death. (The spelling "fauxborg" gives an idea of the original meaning of the modern word "faubourg," false city, or suburb.)

Cole was accompanied by a pushy French servant, for he had found that it was "absolutely necessary to have a French Servant, as [my] own knew not a word of the Language." Unfortunately the fellow was drunk and threw in "impertinent" observations that ruined Cole's experience of going around to look at churches and tourist sights, much as we do today. He was also cheated by his landlady. English mistrust of the French (and vice versa) such as Cole's goes back eternally, or at least to 1066.

Cole described his rooms in some detail, giving a glimpse of what these apartments were like, and though this was a hundred years after d'Artagnan, much would have remained the same:

"... up two Pair of Stairs; it consisted of a little Bedchamber for my Servant in the Passage or little Gallery to my own, ... a Bureau, half a Dozen elegant & sumptuous elbow-Chairs & a Sopha of the same Sort, of the Tapestry of their own Manufacture." He also had an "elegant & lofty Crimson Damask Bed ... raised on a Step," and red tiled or oak floors, heavily waxed, and in general was very comfortable.

For the d'Artagnans all was to end badly; after they had two sons, d'Artagnan began to stray, Madame to nag, and then to have him followed. Finally they parted. She went back to her country place to live, and d'Artagnan went off on the king's wars. Eventually, he would be killed in battle, serving his king.

But he lives on. There are descendants today who can claim him as their ancestor. And most days as I walk up to the Boulevard St.-Germain past the church, a man is standing, dressed as a Musketeer, perhaps d'Artagnan, with leather baldric and high-heeled shoes, shoulder-length hair and wide plumed hat that he is quick to doff while bowing at any queenly figure who comes near enough to toss a euro in his little cup.

THE CHAPEL

*The chances of history are happily reunited in the same
building, conceived by Marguerite—the souvenirs and the
evocations of the Valois, and also of the times which preceded
her intervention in the site, til then empty of inhabitants.*
Emmanuel Schwartz, LA CHAPELLE DE L'ÉCOLE
DES BEAUX-ARTS DE PARIS

My present connection to St.-Germain is for me also
symbolized or represented by something I see out my
kitchen window every day, the back of a little chapel built
by Queen Marguerite de Valois in 1608. It is a building
that d'Artagnan must also have seen, though I cannot
guess whether he ever went inside. Now it can't be seen
at all, either from the street or from within the École des
Beaux-Arts, the national fine arts academy next door.

When we came to live in our apartment on Rue
Bonaparte, I was entranced, and still am, by the things
about it that have not been changed since the seventeenth century—its "Versailles parquet"—which is the

lovely way of laying oak floors in large squares within which the wood is fitted on the diagonal. The windows are twelve feet tall, the ceilings even taller. I even love the gilding on the living room panels, though at first I thought it was gaudy and planned to paint it out. Somehow the eye gets used to decors that in the U.S. would look like hotel lobbies.

In my state of love for my apartment, I hadn't paid attention to the curious, windowless, rounded building about fifteen feet away across a tiny court outside the kitchen window. It was simply there. When I did focus on it, at first I didn't like the dark domed shape, resembling the edge of a huge, lead-colored zeppelin, or perhaps an alien spaceship alighted outside, looming over the small, enclosed garden space, and more than two stories high, covered in slate tiles, overbearing and mysterious.

Nor did I know, at first, what this structure was, though I saw that it was somehow part of the École des Beaux-Arts, an assemblage of buildings built around a vast cobbled court, one of them a church, the others Palladian structures housing classrooms where generations of students—including well-known American artists—have learned architecture or to paint and draw.

I soon learned that the small, rounded structure was somehow part of a church built by Marguerite de Valois or de Navarre—Queen Margot—in 1608. In her day, the tiny chapel stood alone. In seventeenth-century engravings, a small hexagonal structure ornaments her gardens, topped by a cupola and tiny spire. Thirty-five feet across and twenty feet high, it would have been visible from all the paths and walks through her gardens and from her palace nearby. It was her idea that monks would sing there all day long, in praise of God, Jacob, and Jesus, representing her penitence for a misspent life: It was called La Chapelle des Louanges—the Chapel of Praises.

Once freestanding, it now forms a bay of a larger church, Église des Petits-Augustins, which incorporated the chapel when it was built, after 1618. Some time went by until I could go inside either the church or its chapel. At first, I was told by the gatekeeper at the École des Beaux-Arts that though the church would be open for art exhibits from time to time, none was planned for the moment, so I was obliged to look at it, front and back, only from outside. Fortunately, the exterior alone was enough to contemplate in the meantime. There are no windows facing my side, but the front of the church (which is visible in the courtyard of the École des Beaux-Arts) has a tall, flat classical facade taken from the château at Anet of the famous courtesan Diane de Poitiers, about whom more later.

RUE BONAPARTE

*... of which the north part between the Seine and the Rue
Jacob was called chemin de la Petite-Seine (1368), de la
Noue (1523), Rue des Petits-Augustins (XVIIth c.);—the
central part between the Rue Jacob and the boulevard St.-
Germain, open on the ancient abbey, was called Cour des
Religieux (1804), Rue Bonaparte (1810) ...*
Rochegude et Dumolin, GUIDE PRACTIQUE
À TRAVERS LE VIEUX PARIS

My husband John and I have lived on Rue Bonaparte next
to the chapel for about four years now, for six or so months
of every year. Paris comes to feel more and more like home,
while our place in San Francisco seems farther and farther
away. In Paris, we are a step or two away from the Louvre,
the Institut de France, the Pont Neuf, and other iconic
structures in this precious, actually rather small, city.

Rue Bonaparte begins on the Quai Malaquais, on the
Left Bank of the Seine, across from the Louvre. Parisians
make a sharp distinction between the Left and Right

Rue Bonaparte, author's home

Banks of the Seine (by which they mean the south and north banks), but the visitor has the luxury of ignoring this age-old distinction—the legacy of days when the river had to be crossed by ferry—which attributes staid respectability to the Right Bank, and an aura of artiness to the Left. The area is a harmonious ensemble, the work of centuries, but especially of the seventeenth century, the epoch that has most distinctly shaped the whole sixth arrondissement. The eighteenth and nineteenth centuries, and even modern Paris, are also represented within a few minutes' walk, the latter by the new Solférino bridge, a lovely arc linking the Left Bank with the Tuileries, across from the refurbished train station, Gare—now Musée—d'Orsay, a museum for the art of the nineteenth century. The Orsay includes the amazing painting by Courbet, "L'origine du monde," of a hairy vagina and two plump thighs; the eagerness to see this curiosity, I'm told, in part explains the long lines always waiting outside the museum to buy tickets.

And there are vestiges of Roman Paris and medieval Paris within a few minutes' walk. If you go into the parking garage on the Rue Mazarine and walk down one level, you will see a formidable wall, perhaps twenty feet high and six or eight feet thick, of gray stones, part of the wall built by King Philippe-Auguste in 1200 to encircle Paris. Archaeologists must know, but I have never understood, how civilizations sink. They are always covered over by subsequent civilizations, but mustn't they have sunk first, as if the core of the Earth were shrinking, drawing everything down? Or do they rise, thickening the Earth as they acrete layer upon layer of city? It is always hard to visualize.

A few words by way of orientation for anyone who plans walking around. Part of the pleasure of living in Paris is the pleasure of discoveries impossible when you're separated from the world by a car. From Rue Bonaparte I can walk almost anywhere in Paris, and certainly everywhere I need to go. If you want to get there faster, or in bad weather, there are the Métro and the buses, and there is *Paris by Arrondissements,* a little booklet of maps that show every street in every arrondissement. You get it at any newsstand—much easier than unfolding a big map—and with this *indispensable,* and a packet of bus/Métro tickets, or better yet a weekly pass, you can never be lost.

Nor are you in danger, except from pickpockets. It is sometimes hard for visitors to internalize the paradox—having both the carefree feeling that personal safety gives you, and the need to keep your purse and pockets zipped up. I'm both careful and wary, but I do travel a lot, and have been pickpocketed or had things stolen, out of bags, from under the X-ray screener, in a store, five times, always in France. The skill of the pickpockets defies belief. The last time, getting off the bus at my own bus stop, I was so exasperated I confronted the thief and demanded my wallet back. To both our surprise, he gave it to me, without a word, but with a look of fear on his face. Perhaps he (correctly) saw in mine the look of a woman who was going to raise a big, audible fuss.

Say you are standing in the courtyard of the Louvre, the great palace, along with its gardens the Tuileries, that dominates the Right Bank of central Paris (and which any taxi can find). Stand with your back to the Pyramid—the amazing glass structure designed by I. M. Pei when François Mitterand was president. (Mitterand was not the only French president who wanted to change the face of Paris. Luckily most of them have been deterred. One hears that Georges Pompidou, who did place the Centre Pompidou, an amazing modern structure on the site of the old market area, also wanted freeways along the Right and Left Banks. This would have meant tearing down much of historic Paris, rather as Baron Haussmann did in the nineteenth century for Napoleon III, to build the large, handsome Right Bank apartments we think of today as being so typically Parisian.)

Anyway, you are facing the Tuileries. From this spot, you turn left and walk toward the river on the street that runs through the middle of the Louvre, cross the bridge (Pont de Carousel), a wide structure guarded by four female figures, whether queens, goddesses, or muses I am not sure. When you get to the Left Bank turn left on the Quai Malaquais. Walk eastward, crossing the Rue des Sts.-Pères, and continue along the Quai Malaquais past the École des Beaux-Arts museum, a large, classical nineteenth-century building fronting the quay to the next street, which will be Rue Bonaparte. It will take no more than ten minutes to walk from the Louvre to Rue Bonaparte.

On this short stretch of the Quai Malaquais, by the way, the buildings, except for the museum, were built about the time that d'Artagnan came to Paris, in the 1630s. Number seventeen, now part of the École des Beaux-Arts, was formerly Hôtel de la Bazinière, or Chimay, whose beautiful doors are *classées,* that is, on a list of valued buildings or parts of buildings that cannot be changed. We have a friend to whose family this *palais* belonged in former centuries, but I don't know if it was the Revolution or the persecution of Huguenots that deprived them of it.

The name Malaquais came from *mal acquis,* or wrongly acquired, no one knows by whom or why, and the stretch of it between Bonaparte and the Rue des Sts.-Pères was called Escorcherie aux Chevaux. The meaning is unclear—I haven't found the word *escorcherie* in my French dictionary, the closest being *escorter,* to escort. The street names of Paris have often changed when a new or better name came along, and the changes always tell a story. Recently the Quai du Louvre on the Right Bank was changed to Quai François Mitterand after the late president.

As in one of those puzzles where the eye must discern the shapes of cats or Indians from among the patterns in a drawing of draperies or foliage, so do the seventeenth-century houses emerge from the jumble of subsequent construction in St.-Germain, once you start looking for them, for though the quarter is vibrant with modern activities, its characteristic buildings are from the 1600s, and still form the infrastructure of everyday life. The spirit of St.-Germain somehow began with these, and once you are conscious of them, they form the visual matrix as well as the physical foundation, and account for the beauty of the quarter. Here they still are, built around and onto and in front of, but still serviceable and sound, with their gables and pitched roofs, elegant mansards, handsome eaves, and imposing gateways.

Among things Italianate that came with Catherine de Médicis and others in the mid-sixteenth century were architectural principles that influenced the style of most of the great châteaux and palaces of France. The seventeenth-century "hotels" in this neighborhood are classically symmetrical L- or U-shaped buildings set in courtyards, shut off from the street by a wall and gate or by a fourth wall of rooms closing the space so that the courtyard is completely interior, reached by a large street door and wide passage through the streetside building to the court. When the visitor walks along a Paris street he sees a solid facade of buildings with wide, thick oak doors that require numeric codes to be typed in before they will open. He should remember that behind these somber facades are delightful court-yards and gardens, and windows looking down on them as well as onto the street.

Sometimes the garden spaces are enormous—one such garden nearby at 176 Boulevard St.-Germain (serv-ing partly as a parking lot) can be seen by anyone dur-ing the day and gives a good idea of what is often behind the solemn facades. Some of the gardens here and in the seventh arrondissement, belonging to the huge private seventeenth-century palaces, have now been turned into embassies or government buildings, and if you happen to be in Paris on the right weekend in September, all the great private gardens of these buildings, usually hidden, are thrown open to the public. On a subsequent week-end, it is the palaces themselves to be opened, and peo-ple stand in line from early morning to get a glimpse of the remarkable interiors and treasures of furniture and paintings inside, where they are enjoyed by government officials in private the rest of the year.

The gates that wall and close the courtyards are usu-ally high and imposing, large enough for carriages to enter, and sometimes flanked by a single door for entrance by people on foot. (One can't help but think of La Door, the name a witty architectural historian has given to a sort of pretentious door found in fancy Los

Angeles houses; the criterion is that La Door rises higher than the eaves, as these seventeenth-century gates do.) These were palaces designed to announce the wealth, piety, and power of their owners, with vast reception rooms for public entertaining, and smaller, more intimate, apartments above—and with gardens where possible.

The main rooms are on the first floor, that is, to Americans the second floor, or one floor up from street level. These have wooden parquet or stone floors, high ceilings, and tall windows almost to the ceilings, closed by interior shutters or *volets;* the remaining two (usually) floors will have lower ceilings, and on the top floor, the low, small rooms are where the servants lived. Since the invention of the elevator, these rooms have developed considerable prestige, for they are sunny and cozy, and now considered chic. As a result, it's Americans and other foreigners who are consigned to live in the fancy *étages nobles,* apartments unwanted by the French and rented out.

Then, as now, all was and is not grandeur in St.-Germain-des-Prés. On the Rue Visconti, "little Geneva," named after the main center of Protestant thought in Switzerland, runs between Bonaparte and the Rue de Seine. Racine died in 1699 in reduced circumstances at number twenty-four; and Balzac would later have his

Interior of the author's apartment

printing business at number seventeen. These are rather homely buildings, mostly plain-faced stucco over the stone walls, smaller windows shuttered on the outside, with grilles of wrought iron across their lower panes. Throughout the whole of this "historic" area, the city of Paris strictly ordains the color each building is to be painted—no frivolities of rose or blue permitted. Modest expressiveness is allowed in choosing the color of the massive double doors, sometimes painted blue or left in natural wood, like the doors from the château Anet now stuck onto the Église des Petits-Augustins—but the choice for most doors is, overwhelmingly, dark, shiny green.

We, like other foreigners, live on the first floor. At Bonaparte, turn right, and our building is a few doors along on the right, facing number five, which has a battery of plaques announcing that Maréchal Lyautey lived there, and that Edouard Manet was born there in 1832. In four hundred years, any building will have had a lot of residents, its seedy patches and its glorious ones, but number five has had more than its share: The French biographer Henri Troyat lived there until recently; and a friend who grew up in it says that the rumor among its occupants was that Napoleon's

Typical courtyard of the sixth arrondissement

mother did, too, as well as Napoleon's sister, the frisky Pauline Borghese.

Josephine herself lived at 1 Rue Bonaparte with her first husband, Count Beauharnais, who later was beheaded in the Revolution; the street, naturally, wasn't called Rue Bonaparte before Napoleon's time, but Rue des Petits-Augustins. The star of number five has risen these days, as it is partly owned by Pierre Bergé, patron of the arts and founder of the empire of Yves St. Laurent. My friend Monsieur B. says that Bergé, when he wasn't permitted to raise the ceiling of his very grand ground floor apartment, could not be impeded from lowering the floor—but he couldn't confirm this story.

Picture this same Rue Bonaparte at the beginning of the seventeenth century, or still earlier, when it was not a street but a canal, la Petite Seine. The present Rue de Seine was la Grande Seine. Sometime around 1540, la Petite Seine was filled in, and became the Rue des Augustins, or Petits-Augustins, referring to the Augustinian convent being built there, set in the middle of a field, or *pré*. In this field, students from the medieval university used to disport themselves, doing whatever they did, apparently mostly quarrel and fight. A lot of dueling, which seemed to have been the principal activity of the Three Musketeers, went on in this field, and it was here, I was sorry to learn, that the real-life counterpart of Athos, my favorite of the Musketeers, met his real-life end in a duel.

ARRONDISSEMENTS

Rue Bonaparte follows the course of the canal
which fed water from the Seine to the moat surrounding
the abbey of St.-Germain-des-Prés.
GUIDE MICHELIN

The St.-Germain of nostalgic memory is a little smaller than its technical designation by the Ville de Paris, which sees it as bounded by the Seine River; Rues Dauphine and des Grands Augustins on the east (because it would be too bad not to include the huge equestrian statue of Henri IV on the Pont Neuf); the area between the Boulevard St.-Germain and the Rue du Four, up the Rue de Sèvres to the Croix Rouge; and the Rue des Sts.-Pères on the west.

Aristocrats began to build around here in the 1600s on land made fashionable by la Reine Margot, recently divorced from King Henri IV, one of the first influential people to move to the Left Bank, which became easier to get to when the Pont Neuf, a little way upriver, was finished in 1606. The famous guide to the streets of ancient Paris, by J. Hillairet, *Dictionnaire Historique des Rues de Paris,* includes this northern part of Rue Bonaparte in its section on the "Noble Faubourg St.-Germain," presumably because of the great houses such as those at number five and number seven, and those along the quay, along with others in the part of the seventh arrondissement, a little to the west, that also belonged to the great nobles attached to the court.

A good example of the way these seventeenth-century buildings are everywhere nestled among more recent building is Queen Margot's palace itself, what remains of it, at 4-10 Rue de Seine, the next street east of Rue Bonaparte. In the courtyard at number six is the basic building, which now has two more recent wings—a beautiful Renaissance construction, with its raised stone corners and ornamented dormers. To the left in the wall of the courtyard is a passage through which one can see what remains of her garden, still with its enormous chestnut trees. (A paperback edition of Hillairet exists and is by far the most rewarding guidebook to walk around with.)

Rue Bonaparte itself continues southward from where we live, past the ancient church of St.-Germain-des-Prés, across Boulevard St.-Germain, becoming a street of smart shops (mostly clothes, but there is even someone who sells—horrors—ivory), past the Place St.-Sulpice with its strange church and rococco fountain, and finishes at the Jardin du Luxembourg, where Parisians all jog, promenade their babies and dogs, lawn bowl, ride ponies, watch puppet shows, and where Marie de Médicis, the second wife of Henri IV, built her palace, now the French Senate. This southern section of Bonaparte is also included in "St.-Germain-des-Prés," the name to which legends attach, invoking the cafés, artists, elegant lesbians, an atmosphere of intellectual ferment and jazz and so on, though all these seem to have been concentrated in the northern part.

Our Rue Bonaparte apartment is our fourth Paris apartment, each one a little bigger than the last as our bookcases overflow and our family of potential visitors expands with every year. We had no particular intention to live in St.-Germain-des-Prés and were delightfully happy in the fifth arrondissement, where I set my first Paris novels. Frankly, being just plain American, I lack the sensitivities that influence a Parisian's absolute preference for one quarter over another, based on social and real estate calculations that are opaque to mere *étrangers*. All of Paris seems great to me. If I lived in New York, I wouldn't know where I belonged either—West Side? East Side? Village? Anyway, we fell in love with our apartment, and it happened to be in the sixth arrondissement.

St.-Sulpice church and fountain

Real Parisians get attached to their arrondissements and tend to regard moving as unnatural and to be avoided. Rootless Americans, of course, have no such compunctions, but when J. and I moved, first to the fifth arrondissement, and then to the seventh arrondissement, then here to the sixth, each time I felt that I was moving an impossible distance, with all the dislocation to be expected from a large, deracinating life change, as if I had been moving from New York to San Antonio. In fact the fifth arrondissement is an easy walk, or a mere five minutes away on the bus, from where I live now, and there would be no impediment to going back to the same bakery and butcher as always; yet the psychological distance is great. By now perfectly accustomed to my new street, still I often stroll back along the *rive gauche* (south side of the river) to my old neighborhood in the fifth arrondissement, to enjoy the bridges and markets on the way.

Edmund White begins his delightful book about Paris, *The Flâneur,* by noting with satisfaction that Paris is a big city that pleases for its urban texture and the possibilities of anonymity a city affords. This is true enough, but it has also famously and often been observed that Paris is a collection of villages grown together over centuries, which would argue the opposite as the secret of its appeal—that its universally acknowledged charm comes from these diverse origins. The feeling of neighborhood or village right around wherever you live in Paris is one of its greatest charms for a small-town American. As I was raised in an Illinois city of 35,000, in some ways I am more comfortable in the St.-Germain village (which, however, is larger in itself than Moline) than ever I was in exotic California, where I moved in my teens. It is the village-like quality of Paris that has always interested me most, and most affects my life here.

The city has retained a sense of itself as a collection of communities, suburbs, open fields, fortifiable islands—these distinctions preserved in the modern system of arrondissements by which the city is divided into administrative sections, each with its mayor, city hall, and individual character. There is a different feel to, say, the Latin Quarter, with its students and cafés, than to the sixteenth arrondissement, a sumptuous residential quarter with stately nineteenth-century buildings and wide boulevards. The sixth arrondissement, now the most expensive in Paris, clings to its image of boho bookishness.

Probably every corner or block or *place* in Paris has as rich a patina of beautiful buildings, ghosts, murders, joys, the unfolding of strange events, stretching back to Roman times. But since St.-Germain-des-Prés is where we are, every day there comes to my notice some scrap of history or detail of building that I hadn't seen before, reminding that it takes centuries to build this intangible and reassuring aura of complication and permanence that every human psyche seems to need.

Away from America, when I think about my own country, I do wonder if some of our problems are simply those of newness. It almost seems that America today is something like the France of the sixteenth century, torn with religious suspicions, cultural divisions, a huge gulf between rich and poor, dangerous streets, and so on. Today, on Rue Bonaparte, the seventeenth-century buildings, neatly polished and painted, lean serenely against each other or rock backward on their heels, tossed and aslant as the ground beneath them has sunk and settled into its tunnels and underground streams, here to stay.

And since there are as many Parises as there are people who live or visit, so there are as many beginnings, each personal and cherished, by which each visitor comes to feel a sort of connection here. What other place has such a resonance with each soul who walks around in it, choosing his personal selection of sites and sights, building a complex and (usually) satisfying set of memories to take away, even if the memories include heartbreak, as in those American stories I mentioned? For the moment, though, J. and I lead the quiet daily lives of real Parisians, even though we will always be foreigners, comfortable in the knowledge that being a stranger is in itself very much in the tradition of St.-Germain-des-Prés. Since long before those Italian queens arrived in the sixteenth century, it is, and has been, the haven of people from everywhere else.

QUEEN MARGOT

*The bride was the daughter of Henry II, the pearl
of the crown of France, Marguerite de Valois, whom,
in his familiar tenderness for her, King Charles IX
always called* ma soeur *Queen Margot.
Marguerite at this period was scarcely twenty,
and already she was the object of all the poets' eulogies,
some of whom compared her to Aurora, others to Cytherea.*
Alexandre Dumas, LA REINE MARGOT

One of several Italian queens of France, Catherine de
Médicis, had a daughter, the Reine Margot, Queen
Marguerite de Valois, later Marguerite de Navarre, who
was in some ways the founder of the neighborhood.
Margot was not one of the better-known queens of
France, but now I think she is one of the most fascinating, and for me the presiding genius of the bookish and
worldly quarter St.-Germain-des-Prés began to become,
once it was liberated from the stern monks of the abbey
of St.-Germain-des-Prés. These latter had been here for

a thousand years, presiding over peasant festivals like the giant Foire de St.-Germain-des-Prés (a sort of precursor of state fairs and the like, known for pickpockets then as now), settling scholarly disputes, conducting diplomacy, and meting out justice.

Marguerite de Valois lived from 1553 to 1615 (approximately contemporary with Shakespeare); and she lived more or less on this spot; our building stands in what was her gardens, and I have mentioned her palace only a few minutes' walk from here, on what is now Rue de Seine. Queen Margot in many ways seems to have set the tone of St.-Germain-des-Prés, of music, intellectual life, adultery, and massacres, to say nothing of starting the real estate boom, as one of the first royal persons of importance to live on this side of the river (the great princes had long lived nearly within earshot across the river at the Louvre).

Seventeenth- and eighteenth-century portraits never succeed in conveying to our modern eyes the charms of fabled beauties. Ladies in old portraits are apt to seem to us too stout, somewhat chinless, their eyes a bit bulging, their hair too elaborate. How much this is owing to techniques of portraiture and how much to changing standards of beauty is hard to say. Queen Margot's beauty is not especially obvious from her picture, and she was the daughter of Catherine de

Médicis; probably any daughter of this illustrious queen would automatically be agreed to possess beauty, whatever the case. Her portraits show an intelligent, quizzical lady, slender, with her breasts thrust up with a kind of Wonder Bra effect from under her low bodice, wearing the ruff and wide skirts we associate with Queen Elizabeth of England.

Queen Margot was described by Dumas, who was drawing on older accounts, as "comely," "the pearl of the crown of France," with black hair (someone else says chestnut), a voluptuous figure, and very small feet, an attribute he seems to have admired and often awarded to his heroines. (In the 1993 Chereau film made from Dumas's novel *La Reine Margot,* she is played by normal-footed Isabelle Adjani.) A few details about her life: She was the child of Catherine de Médicis and the Valois king Henri II, born at the royal château at St.-Germain-en-Laye, christened Marguerite, and nicknamed Margot.

Catherine de Médicis (or de Medici, or d'Medici) was the formidable Italian queen who is said to have brought ice cream, an Italian expertise at poisoning, and various other Renaissance fashions with her to France when she married Henri II, himself son of the great King François I. Catherine de Médicis seems to have been a terrifying mother—manipulative, competitive, and sly, at least where her daughter Margot was concerned, though Margot wrote of her mildly enough, "The Queen my mother [was] a woman endowed with the greatest prudence and foresight of anyone I ever knew."

Catherine was a dangerous enemy, though she doted on all of her king sons: François II—the boy who was married at the age of fourteen to Mary Queen of Scots but died when he was sixteen; Charles IX, the brother of whom Queen Margot was fondest; and Henri III, who was her bitter foe. A sister, Elisabeth, was married to the king of Spain, Philip II, and another to the Duke of Lorraine. All told, Catherine de Médicis produced ten children with Henri II, despite his constant attendance on his mistress, the "ancient" Diane de Poitiers. Some said that one of the roles of this mistress was just to get Henri in the mood for his marital duties.

In 1572, when Margot was nineteen, her mother arranged for her to be given in a marriage of state to Henri of Navarre, the young king of the region of Navarre, and a Huguenot, that is, a Protestant. The idea was to create harmony between Catholics and Huguenots after a long period of bloody sectarian wars during the 1500s.

Some might have thought that nineteen was a bit old for a woman to get married in those days, but Margot hadn't been wasting her time: she had been what would now be called "sexually active" since she was fifteen or sixteen, and she'd planned on marrying her lover, the Duc de Guise. She was also offered to the king of Portugal, negotiations that broke down, and to Don Carlos, the son of the king of Spain. Was it her damaged reputation that put these princes off?

In any case, at the wedding the groom and bride were both sulky, and Queen Margot had to be made to nod her assent. History doesn't record anything about the wedding night. Dumas invents a sort of *mariage blanc* pact between them: "I do not ask you to love me— but if you will be my ally, I could brave everything," he has Henry tell Queen Margot, but her memoirs suggest that there was something between them. She talks about times when they have fallen out and have separate beds, implying that sometimes they slept together, and even long after the events she is relating, when she tells about some of her husband's love affairs, her tone is still one of injured pique.

Whatever their private rapport, six days after the wedding, Queen Margot's brother, King Charles IX, and her mother Catherine de Médicis instigated or acceded to a terrible massacre, in which huge numbers of Protestants were slaughtered, in the Louvre, in central Paris, and all around France.

ST.-BARTHOLOMEW'S DAY

The King of Navarre remained a prisoner in the Louvre
while the pursuit of the Huguenots went on hotter than ever.
To the terrible night had succeeded a day of massacre still
more horrible.

Alexandre Dumas, LA REINE MARGOT

The massacre of St.-Bartholomew's Day happened as follows: Henri's Huguenot followers had been invited to
Paris for his wedding to Margot. As Dumas tells it,
"The spacious apartments of the Louvre were filled with
those brave Protestants to whom the marriage of their
young leader Henri promised an unexpected return of
good fortune" after the protracted religious wars that
had occupied France in the sixteenth century, when
Martin Luther's reforms continued to spread with fierce
enthusiasm over Europe, entangled with the larger
geopolitical ambitions of both Spain and England.

Henri of Navarre, Queen Margot's reluctant husband,
was ruler of a region which lay in both today's Spain

and France in the Pyrenees. His fiercely Huguenot and militant mother Jeanne d'Albret had recently died, so he had became the nominal head of the Protestant faction. As befits a romantic hero, Henri, at least in Dumas's novel, had "a keen eye, black hair cut very close, thick eyebrows, and a nose curved like an eagle's" and he was about the same age as his bride, nineteen.

Henri and his companions were mistaken about forthcoming good fortune. On the night of August 24, 1572, Catholic partisans of Catherine de Médicis and Charles IX by prearrangement fell upon and began slaughtering Protestants, initiating a period of violence in which, by some estimates, thirty thousand people were killed throughout France. Some estimates are higher.

Writing about the massacre later, Queen Margot's account tends to excuse certain aspects of it that seem especially infamous, especially the part played by her brother Charles IX, of whom she was fond, tending to blame it on her mother: Charles, "a prince of great prudence," and "always paying a particular deference to his mother," and "being much attached to the Catholic religion," agreed to do as Catherine urged and dispose of the Protestants. "Immediately every hand was at work; chains were drawn across the streets, the alarm-bells were sounded, and every man repaired to his post, according to the orders he had received."

The newly married Margot was not told what was going on. The Huguenots were suspicious of her because she was a Catholic, and the Catholics because she had married a Huguenot. "This being the case, no one spoke a syllable of the matter to me," she writes later. As the massacre was getting underway, she went in to say good night to her mother, and found her sister in tears. Catherine de Médicis abruptly told Margot to go to bed, but her sister said "for the love of God, do not stir out of this chamber." This earned the sister a severe rebuke from their mother.

"My sister replied it was sending me away to be sacrificed; for, if any discovery should be made, I should be the first victim of their revenge. The Queen my mother made answer that, if it pleased God, I should receive no hurt, but it was necessary I should go, to prevent the suspicion that might arise from my staying."

Apparently Henri of Navarre observed the custom of other kings by going to bed in a public way surrounded by courtiers. When Margot got to her room, Henri sent for her; and she found him already in bed, with thirty or forty of his men around the bed, all of them talking about the attempted assassination of a prominent Huguenot admiral by—Queen Margot does not go into this—her former lover de Guise. It appears the Protestants didn't at first realize what was happening outside the Louvre, where the vicious slaughter was beginning.

Henri was in effect a prisoner, but was given a chance to convert to Catholicism, and gracefully did, thus escaping death on the spot. But he was confined to the Louvre. Eventually, with Queen Margot's help, he would escape and leave the area, and Queen Margot, still suspected by him for her Catholicism and by her family because she was married, thanks to them, to him, continued to be imprisoned for some time in her quarters at the Louvre.

HUGUENOTS

What did God do before He created the world?
He created Hell, for the curious.

JOHN CALVIN

The sixth arrondissement, right around Rue Bonaparte, was the scene of much of the slaughter. This area was something of a Protestant enclave, "little Geneva." The first Protestant synod in France had been held in the Rue Visconti in secret in 1555. The abbey of St.-Germain itself, under Abbot Guillaume Briconnet, was one of the first places to begin to entertain reformist ideas in the days of Luther, and gather "humanists" around. The Protestant center and library are still in the place of the former grand mansion of Salomon de Brosse, the architect of the Luxembourg Palace, at 54 Rue des Sts.-Pères, who was buried in a Protestant cemetery on the same street until the revocation of the Edict of Nantes.

The sixteenth century, when Marguerite and Henri were born (1553), had been one of constant religious turmoil, a clash of several civilizations—between Protestants and Catholics, and between popular and aristocratic forces, this turmoil one of the more convincing parallels with our own times. Martin Luther had been born in Germany in 1483, and by the early 1500s his protest had spread throughout France and into Italy, Spain, and the Low Countries. The astonishing speed with which Luther's ideas and popular appeal caught on is explained by one commentator as because he was the "articulate voice of latent, slumbering nationalism." That is, there was as much or more of politics as of doctrine behind the rise of Protestantism, in that people everywhere were fed up with the greedy kings that ruled them, and also with the abuses they suffered at the hands of the imperious and expensive popes. It's always hard to sort out principle and expedience, which often feel the same to those that hold them.

How Protestantism could so quickly invade and divide France is the question. Certainly it had French roots— John Calvin had studied in Paris—but the royal family, with its Italian connections, was staunchly Catholic. France was still a collection of fiefdoms and small kingdoms ruled by the Bourbons in Navarre, the Duke of Lorraine, and dozens of other what we might now call warlords. The rulers of France were far from secure in forging a nation, let alone imposing religious solidarity. Yet some estimates say that half the French nobility became Protestant in the 1560s (at one point or another, given that conversions were easily reversible in those days).

Conversion seems to have especially appealed to the nobility and prosperous bourgeoisie, who had the most to lose to the Church, and therefore to gain from the new religion. Queen Margot, looking back on her girlhood, when Luther's teachings began to interest people in France, noted that at the time she was seven or eight, the "whole Court was infected with heresy, about the time of the Conference of Poissy. It was with great difficulty that I resisted and preserved myself from a change of religion at that time."

Courtiers tried to convert her, and did almost succeed in temporarily converting her brother the Duc d'Anjou, later King Henri III of France. He would snatch her prayer books and burn them, and give her books of Huguenot prayers, which she would give to her nanny, a "steadfast" Catholic. Henri would threaten that she'd get a whipping if she didn't convert; "Well, get me whipped if you can; I will suffer whipping, and even death, rather than be damned," she claims to have said.

A political explanation for the appeal of Protestantism makes more sense than an entirely theological one—it is hard to see that anyone would be fired up by the idea of, say, Election, the unpleasant notion introduced by John

Calvin that you went to heaven or were damned according to God's plan for you, never mind how good or pious you were. This discouraging idea and others in both religions were hardly to be welcomed, but the underlying political realities may have made them convenient when it came to self-justification. On the other hand, noted historians have also pointed out that people must have also been sincere: "Only religion could unite the divergent interests of nobles, bourgeois and peasants over an area as large as France" (R. J. Knecht, *The French Religious Wars, 1562–1598*).

Max Weber has pointed out that conveniently for Protestants, a recommended method of dispersing religious doubt and allaying religious anxiety was "intense worldly activity." Moneymaking was one such worldly activity, and military conquest was another. Both were appealing features of the new beliefs. Art, interestingly enough, seemed to have been a third activity: a number of architects (Salomon de Brosse), painters, sculptors, and craftsmen like the tapestry-maker Gobelin, or the potter Bernard Palissy, who was eventually martyred, were Protestants, drawn to it perhaps because of the more subjective and interior nature of artistic work.

In fact, it is strangely hard, reading French history, to find out who was and wasn't a Protestant, even among the more visible figures of the period, as if historical tact forbids the mention of a slightly unmentionable quality, like a disease. Even the Bibliothèque Protestante doesn't have a list of seventeenth-century followers, maybe because for a long time, it was dangerous to profess this faith and people didn't keep lists. Yet Catholic-Protestant disputes animated the major political events for centuries.

Long before the St.-Bartholomew's Day crisis, Queen Margot's mother, Catherine de Médicis, regent for her son the young Charles IX, and a prudent Italian strategist, had been worrying about the divisive effects for France of religious quarrels, and had convened a conference at Poissy in September 1561 between Protestants and Catholics in an attempt to resolve doctrinal matters and avert threatened military conflict. The conference was unsuccessful; the talks collapsed on the issues of the Eucharist and the role of the pope, two things that still divide the two religions today. The wars began, and Queen Margot and her little brother, the Duc d'Alençon, were taken for safety to the beautiful château of Amboise (still to be seen; it was here that Mary Stuart and her young husband had watched with glee the hanging of Protestants from the battlements). Many ladies of the court went with Margot and her brother, including one duchess who, Queen Margot later noted, had "the good fortune to hear there of the death of her brute of a husband, killed at the battle of

Dreux. The husband I mean was the first she had, named d'Annebaut, who was unworthy to have for a wife so accomplished and charming a woman."

The slightly facetious tone is typical of her.

Many people were hidden in and around the abbey of St.-Germain during the days of the massacre and the pogroms that would follow at intervals throughout the next century. I've been told that behind our guest-room wall, there are the vestiges of a little staircase leading to a hiding space where Jews were hidden during the Second World War—perhaps Protestants, too, during some earlier time? Some day I mean to uncover the staircase, but meantime can't figure out where it could be, and, frankly, it does seem that if people had been hidden in all the hiding spaces now claimed in Paris, there would have been no one sent to his death in the camps, as we know happened; is it a bit like the beds Washington, or Napoleon, slept in?

But the myth of virtuous humanitarianism masks the violent facts. It is sure that it was near Rue Bonaparte, in the garden of the old prison of the abbey, that 372 people—aristocrats and priests detained in the Revolution—were massacred in 1792. Here, as everywhere in France during the Second World War,

Jews were made to wear yellow stars, until the day they vanished. There was the Nazi occupation, the effects of which we see in the touching plaques set everywhere in walls around Paris, to mark the place where someone was killed.

LE DIVORCE

*When we have grown tired of loving, we are delighted
at the other's unfaithfulness, for that releases
us from having to be faithful.*

François de La Rochefoucauld, MAXIM #581

A word or two more about Queen Margot's history, leading up to the construction of the Chapel of Praises outside
my kitchen window. Blood relations seemed not entirely
to protect an individual in the chancy circles of a sixteenth-century court. Though she was the daughter of a
king of France (Henri II), the (eventually divorced) wife of
a king of France (Henri IV), and the sister of three kings
of France (Charles IX, Henri III, and François II), in the
years after her marriage, poor Margot was often imprisoned or exiled at the whim of one of her brothers, even of
her mother, who had promoted her loveless marriage of
state. In 1586, she was imprisoned or exiled by her brother Henri III in the castle of Usson, in Auvergne, there to
improve her mind, write her memoirs, compose music,

and generally pass the time for eighteen years, although not without a lover, the Marquis de Canillac, who was supposed to be guarding her.

Apropos of this, it was always said of her that she was "lascivious"—Joseph Boniface de La Mole, Jacques de Harlay, Seigneur de Chanvallon, and Bussy d'Amboise are among those listed by historians among her lovers at this time. (The latter was also the boyfriend of her brother Henri.) It does seem that queens are often said to be lascivious—those who are not held to be pious. It's hard to know how much is just part of the traditional mythology of queens. It was said of Marie-Antoinette, probably unfairly, and with better foundation of Catherine the Great, to name two. On the whole, it's the lascivious queens who seem better remembered. Perhaps it is just that queens are appointed to behave representatively, living the way ordinary people would like to, at least when it comes to lasciviousness and vengeful fantasies.

In the lives of queens, probably, much is legend. Like Puccini's Turandot, Queen Margot was also said to have had lovers executed who didn't please her (think too of Elizabeth I and the Earl of Essex), and even, *bien sûr,* to have preserved their hearts and/or heads, as she promises to do, in Dumas's novel, with those of her lover La Mole after his execution, and as Mme. de Rénal does with the head of Julien Sorel in Stendhal's *The Red and the Black*. Perhaps it was some special French fascination with heads that led them to invent the guillotine?

Writing was one consolation during her exile at Usson; and it seems she had literary visitors, among them Michel de Montaigne, whose own writings were perhaps another consolation. Earlier, when she had been confined to her apartments in the Louvre, she reported that she "had found a secret pleasure, from the perusal of good books, to which I have given myself up with a delight I never before experienced. I consider this an obligation I owe to fortune, or, rather to Divine Providence, in order to prepare me, by such efficacious means, to bear up against the misfortunes and calamities that awaited me."

Eventually, leading the religious/political faction at his command, her husband Henri would go back to Protestantism, then turn Catholic again when he became King Henri IV, succeeding Margot's brother Henri III as king of France. That was when he made his famous remark that *"Paris vaut bien une messe"*—Paris was well worth going to Mass a few times.

In 1592, negotiations were begun to dissolve his marriage to Margot. Was it because, like Henry VIII of

England, he wanted to remarry, because of childlessness, or because they didn't get along? It would take seven years, until 1599, but eventually, the marriage was annulled, preparing the way for Henri to marry Marie de Médicis, another Italian import, who would be mother of Louis XIII, beginning that string of Louises that ended with the beheading of Louis XVI during the Revolution, or in fact with the end of the reign of Louis XVIII in 1824. Marie would herself rule for her young son after Henri IV was assassinated, another of the female regents in French history.

In return for her cooperation with the divorce, Margot got an agreement that allowed her to keep the title of queen, and a promise that Henri would pay her debts; Henri would become one of France's best-remembered kings, among other things for issuing the Edict of Nantes, ensuring civil rights and toleration for the Huguenots, and therefore civil harmony which lasted until Louis XIV, who revoked it and canceled toleration in 1685.

Queen Margot remained a well-liked ex-queen. She got along with her ex-husband and his new wife, Marie de Médicis, and threw herself into arts and good works, was nice to the children of the new couple (she appears not to have produced any legal heirs herself, though accounts vary as to whether she had other children), and generally behaved as a benevolent aunt or godmother. She's accessible to us because she wrote her memoirs, discreet and incomplete though they are, revealing all the same:

"Misfortune prompts us to summon our utmost strength to oppose grief and recover tranquillity, until at length we find a powerful aid in the knowledge and love of God, whilst prosperity hurries us away until we are overwhelmed by our passions," she wrote, in the uncharacteristically resigned tone that sometimes crept into her writing during her long exile.

She began construction of the Chapel of Praises in 1608, once she had returned to Paris after the eighteen years in Usson. Usually headstrong, she began building in one of her pious and penitent phases, though her memoirs break off before she can recount this Paris part of her personal history. After her long isolation, her life became a novel, as the French say: *Ma vie est un roman*—a novel about the relative consolations of religion and license. Already in her fifties when she moved back to Paris, she piled up new lovers and new debts. The story is told of one of her young lovers killing another at her very door, and being executed the next day under her window.

It was then she fled from the Marais (where she had lived in the vast and gloomy medieval Hôtel de Sens), bought a large tract of land on the Left Bank, built a splendid house on the Rue de Seine, laid out her gardens, and eventually began to build La Chapelle des Louanges, or Chapel of Praises, in whose shadow John and I are living now. The chapel and our buildings were in what were the vast gardens of her estate—the Rue Jacob, for instance, was one of the *allées* of this garden. Nearby, her ex-husband Henri was constructing the Place Dauphine on the Île de la Cité. His is the giant equestrian statue you see as you cross the Pont Neuf.

In the chapel, monks of the Petits-Augustins were to offer up songs of her own composing around the clock to fulfill her vows, till she got tired of it, for she was both musical and literary, as well as renowned for her love affairs. The singing, indeed the chapel itself, was intended as part of her vow to Jacob, he of the ladder, to atone for what she began to feel had been a too-worldly life—learned, lascivious, and pious at different times, and sometimes all at once, like many people. Eventually, it is said, she became very stout.

D'Artagnan's Paris

D'Artagnan therefore entered Paris on foot,
carrying his small valise under his arm, and proceeded
until he found a lodging suitable to his slender resources.
This chamber was a sort of garret, situated in the
Rue des Fossoyeurs, near the Luxembourg.
Alexandre Dumas, THE THREE MUSKETEERS

Queen Margot had outlived her ex-husband Henri IV and all of her family, and died in the year of d'Artagnan's birth, 1615, leaving her land to her ex-husband's son Louis XIII, who set out to liquidate her considerable debts. In the twenty years between Queen Margot's death and d'Artagnan's arrival in Paris, her palace on the Rue de Seine had been sold off in three parts, two of which remain today, one at number 10 and 10 bis (where Rosa Bonheur would teach drawing two centuries later); another at numbers 8-6; while the remainder, at 2-4, "disappeared," *disparu,* that wonderfully nonjudgmental and ambiguous French word: in this case, torn down.

Sometimes on my walks, I try to imagine the neighborhood as d'Artagnan would have seen it when he came to Paris as a very young man, probably around 1635, to join the king's guards. After Queen Margot's death, Louis XIII had divided her land into lots and sold parcels to developers, in the modern way, and in no time the neighborhood was a fever of building, either of sumptuous private residences to live in, or to sell or rent for profit. Aristocrats and the successful rich began to move over to the Left Bank in greater numbers, and the quarter got much of the look it has today. On Rue Bonaparte, certainly the building next door to us at 6 Rue Bonaparte, and the low building at number two were here by d'Artagnan's day. The latter, which dates from the early seventeenth century, houses a frame shop that used to be called "Paris-American Art," but which has now painted out the word "American," for fear of anti-American reprisals. (They say they'll paint it back some day. Maybe.) There remains the question about our building and numbers ten and twelve: When were they built?

D'Artagnan certainly knew the most important monument of the quarter, the church of St.-Germain-des-Prés, at the corner of Rue Bonaparte and the Boulevard St.-Germain, where it has stood in some form or another since the sixth century, some think on the site of a first-century Roman altar. In d'Artagnan's day

Church of St.-Germain-des-Prés

it was a powerful abbey, mostly dating from the twelfth century, with extensive grounds where he and others fought duels.

It had been consecrated in 558 by a Merovingian king, Childebert I, the son of Clovis. At first it was called St.-Vincent-et-St.-Croix, after St.-Vincent, relics of whom Childebert had brought back from an expedition against the Visigoths in Spain; but by the eighth century it had taken the name of St.-Germain, after the early cardinal Germain who had inspired its building and was buried inside, along with Clovis and subsequent kings. Hillairet, the indispensable index to Parisian streets, says that the "des-Prés" was added to distinguish this church from another, St.-Germain-le-Vieux.

The Normans sacked the church in the ninth century; it was rebuilt in about the year 1000—the "incipiently Gothic" features of the choir were designed, perhaps by the architect of the cathedral at Sens, about 1145. After that, chapels and cloisters were added over the centuries, dismantled yet again, rebuilt yet again. In 1794, during the Revolution, when religion was disapproved of, it was used to store gunpowder, and accidentally blew up, destroying the refectory, the Chapel of the Virgin, and its immense library, though many of the manuscripts were saved. After that, the whole wreck was in danger of being demolished, but was rescued by Victor Hugo, among others, who led a campaign to save it. Thus it was rebuilt another time, but never did get back two of its original three towers.

During the time of its ascendancy, this church and abbey were rich and powerful, answerable only to the pope—or perhaps not even to the pope—and in effect governed the surrounding population. It owned extensive lands, for the use of which it exacted revenues, was a center of learning in competition with and in frequent dispute with the Sorbonne, and even had political powers of taxing and punishing misdeeds, for which, the prison.

Now it still forms the centerpiece of the neighborhood, as it has for a thousand years, but it stands alone in a setting of worldly consumerism and mundane big-city bustle, across from the boutiques of Louis Vuitton and Christian Dior, and a building that houses The Society for Encouragement of Industry. The irony of this unholy atmosphere of commerce escapes no one, and is especially emphasized by the current mode at Dior, of bruised biker-moll clothes, spike heels and punk chains, a sort of celebration of depravity chic that would have shocked the abbots, and probably elegant old Christian Dior himself as well.

"On Sundays we sat at the Deux Magots and watched the people, devout as an opera chorus, enter the old doors,"

At Les Deux Magots

wrote Zelda Fitzgerald in the twenties; but signs of devoutness are long gone. People sitting on the terrace of Les Deux Magots, gazing out at the church in good weather (rare in Paris), behold in the forecourt an antic crowd of musicians, many of them Americans, doing familiar jazz chestnuts and endless renditions of "As the Saints Go Marching In"; the mime dressed up like d'Artagnan; the little old woman who does Piaf imitations very badly almost every night; the waffleseller; a man who pretends to paint tiny postcard-size pictures of local sights; and dozens of other characters. I haven't seen the organ-grinder lately, with his family of docile or drugged cats.

The Place St.-Germain-des-Prés is cobbled with largish stones, terrible in high heels as you run for the 63 Bus across the boulevard. Concerts are held in the church many nights of the week, heavily emphasizing Vivaldi's *Four Seasons*. All in all, there is a festival quality to the precincts of the ancient church that must be somewhat like that of medieval times. It makes a rather profane sight, so that the simple white cross erected over the porch is startling as the solitary reference to higher things.

The church does still have its ritual and ceremonial functions. Just after September 11, 2001, people gathered there for a silent prayer vigil. Those who came were not just Americans—there were many French people, too, and some people who looked like North Africans, that is, Muslims. Almost every American who was here on that day talks about the support and concern Paris felt, and experienced some expression of kindness and sympathy. In my building, two of my neighbors offered guest bedrooms and haven to anyone we might know stranded in France because of the interruption of transatlantic travel. What changes have taken place between our two nations in two years! But the French, at least, assure Americans it isn't us, only our leader, that they mistrust.

Inside the church, which, to be frank, is not as beautiful or moving as many churches, the most affecting thing is the chapel of St.-Symphorian, a simple stone-walled space dating from the eighth century, accessible through double doors on the right-hand side of the porch. Symphorian was a young Roman soldier, martyred in the first century, but for what not even Google seems to know, presumably Christianity.

If you walk along the Rue de l'Abbaye, the street that runs just north of the church of St.-Germain-des-Prés, and which was not there in d'Artagnan's day, first you see a little square park, Square Laurent-Prache, which snuggles up to the side of the church, and contains in the space of a few hundred square yards allusions to all the long history of St.-Germain-des-Prés. To begin, someone has scrawled on a bas-relief of the worthy gentleman Laurent Prache, whoever he was, after whom the square is named, "tête du con," meaning, more or less, "what an asshole," a typical graffitist sentiment, a little jarring for this churchly precinct, but modern in feeling.

Elsewhere in the little garden of the square, which can't be more than sixty feet on each side, a statue of Dora Maar by Picasso, and dedicated by him to his friend Apollinaire, sits on a pedestal, and bits of the thirteenth-century chapel of the Virgin are stuck to the outside walls of the church, saved from further depredations but deteriorating in the polluted air. After the Revolution, when everything was for sale, a local doctor bought the damaged chapel and tore it down to reuse the bits to decorate his house. His house was in turn torn down—*sic transit Gloria*—and the fragments came back to be displayed here. The bust of Dora Maar was stolen a couple of years ago, too, but recovered under circumstances that remain a little mysterious. At least she is back, though some say this bust is a copy, and the Ville de Paris is tight-lipped about the whole affair.

As you continue down Rue de l'Abbaye, there are more bits of ancient buildings preserved as parts of the structures of several boutiques across the street from the abbatial palace, in Flamant, a furniture store, for example, where they form part of the wall of the building, and in the shop that sells things from Asia at number ten, in a *sous-sol* that can be seen from the street through the window. At the end of the street on the right, the abbot's palace, built in 1586, still looks rather as it must have looked to d'Artagnan, built of brick and stone in the style seen in the Place des Vosges in the fourth arrondissement. Its size gives a good idea of the power and influence of the abbots of St.-Germain—it appears nearly as large as the church itself, its grounds still luxuriously ample, and it seems still to belong to the Catholic Church.

From here, turn left and walk through the charming Place de Furstemburg to Rue Jacob, another street so charged with history, so overlain with the names of all the famous people who had lived there that it almost baffles description. At number three, for example, just to the right when you reach Jacob, was the eighteenth-century home of the unfortunate Princesse de Lamballe, the friend of Marie-Antoinette who was dismembered by an angry mob, and her body parts gleefully paraded outside the queen's prison window. I have two different American friends who are living at 3 Jacob now, one of them in an apartment that used to belong to Simonetta, the Italian dress designer (who still lives elsewhere on Rue Jacob), and the other who rents from a French baroness. And so on, up the entire street, haunt of Tom Paine, Franklin, Washington Irving, Hemingway ...

The Rue des Fossoyeurs, where d'Artagnan found his first Paris lodging, came to be called Rue Servandoni in 1806. I like to think he could have been renting in the house of Madame D.—a wonderful guru to artists, to whom I once in desperation repaired for a (miraculous) consultation, whose family (Protestant) has lived there since the seventeenth century. The ironwork on her stairs is the same as in our building, perhaps another clue to the date of ours.

END OF THE GREAT CENTURY

Whatever great advantages nature may give,
it is not she alone, but fortune also that makes the hero.

François de La Rochefoucauld

The seventeenth century drew on. D'Artagnan died in
1672. He had served Louis XIII, and in turn Louis XIV,
the Sun King, but with the latter, the court had moved
off to Versailles, and Rue Bonaparte resumed a calmer
aspect. St.-Germain was fashionable now for its graceful
social life, wit, and literary bent, the character it would
keep, interspersed with periods of catastrophe.

I think of the Duc de La Rochefoucauld as the emblem-
atic man for this time—sometime around 1660 he lived
near here in the house of his uncle, on the Rue de Seine
(14-18 Rue de Seine), a few hundred yards from where
Queen Margot's palatial residence had been. His pious and
talented friend Madame de La Fayette lived not far away
on Rue Vaugirard, other friends were a bit farther away
at Port-Royal, a neighborhood at the south of the sixth

arrondissement, at the border of the fifth (twenty minutes' walk from here), immersed in the mood of the Jansenists. These devout crypto-Protestant Catholics reacted to the power and political status of the Church by encouraging private devotions, translations of the Bible, a return to simple forms of worship, and so on—a movement so menacing to Louis XIV, perhaps for the subtly seditious political implications of these criticisms of Jesuit and pope, that he had the convent of the Port-Royal nuns burned to the ground.

The sixth Duc de La Rochefoucauld was born in 1613 (two years before d'Artagnan), and had the career expected of a man in his position: He joined the army, was involved in most of the going conspiracies against Cardinals Richelieu and Mazarin, participated in the Fronde—an uprising of aristocrats against Mazarin— was wounded in battle, exiled, and jailed, but survived to end his days peacefully enough in Paris in a circle of his friends, including Madame de Sévigné, Madame de La Fayette, whose *La Princesse de Cleves* is thought of as almost the first and among the greatest of French novels, and his particular friend, Madame de Sablé. These were stately, or it could seem, mildly depressed, intellectuals who found solace in each other, in literature, and in witty topical dissections. In short, they had *salons,* a social form that had begun in the sixteenth century, and still characterized this period. With their famous interdiction of talk about politics and religion (respected to our day, if more in the breach than the observance, given everyone's actual preoccupation with politics and religion) they were, after the court, major arbiters of taste.

They valued concise expression, purity of feeling, wit, and affection, but it was the barbed and even bitter mockery of La Rochefoucauld's tone that would be widely adopted, even become characteristic in the eighteenth century with Voltaire, Madame de Stael, and so on. The salons gave considerable influence to women. The seventeenth-century salons, many of them around Port-Royal, must have lent to this whole quarter the sort of tone that would persist in the 1920s when American and English women, many of them lesbian or black, would find a congenial atmosphere of female self-sufficiency.

La Rochefoucauld's epigrams convey the mood of the upcoming eighteenth century: harsh but undeniable, startling in the hypocrisies they exposed:

Whatever care we take to conceal our passions under the appearance of piety and honor, they are always to be seen through these veils.

Our virtues are most frequently but vices in disguise.

His maxims brilliantly characterize the dodgy life of a courtier:

Hypocrisy is the homage vice pays to virtue.

We promise according to our hopes; we perform according to our fears.

Interest speaks all sorts of tongues and plays all sorts of characters; even that of disinterestedness.

He is always preoccupied with death, with a very modern skepticism:

Men have written in the most convincing manner to prove that death is no evil, and this opinion has been confirmed on a thousand celebrated occasions by the weakest of men as well as by heroes. Even so I doubt whether any sensible person has ever believed it, and the trouble men take to convince others as well as themselves that they do shows clearly that it is not an easy undertaking.

By the end of the seventeenth century, La Rochefoucauld is dead (1680), as is Madame de La Fayette (who said of him, "He gave me wit, I gave him a heart.") in 1692, and Madame de Sévigné (1696), too. The latter two ladies lived to see Louis XIV revoke the Edict of Nantes, and the country plunged again into religious turmoil, with an enormous exodus of Protestants to Holland, England, and the New World. (According to my aunts, one of our ancestors went to America soon after, one René Cossé or Cosset, whose name in the more dubiously educated colonies became "Ranna Cossit." Was he a Huguenot? My aunt doesn't know.)

No more do I know about La Rochefoucauld's religion. Having become interested in Huguenots, despite the mysterious silence about which historical figures were and weren't Protestants, I still find myself wondering who was who in this respect. Even in accounts of, for instance, the Fronde, the rebellions against Louis XIV and Mazarin that La Rochefoucauld fought in, though the Fronde involved many of the same families as in the former Huguenot period, no religious concerns are implied, at least that are apparent to the casual reader. (Leonard Tancock, introducing his translation of La Rochefoucauld's *Maxims,* says of the Fronde: "Its events were industriously obscured by the memoirs and special pleadings of many of the participants, and no attempt has been made here to unravel the skein.") Yet La Rochefoucauld's great-grandfather died in the massacre of St.-Bartholomew's Day. That earlier La Rochefoucauld was certainly a Huguenot, chief henchman of Jeanne d'Albret, the mother of Henri IV. Would not his memory be alive in the La Rochefoucauld family a mere hundred years later? Several at least of the leading Frondists were raised as Protestants, yet lurking religious rancor is not seen as having anything to do with their opposition to the two influential cardinals or any royal personages. At the least, people like La Rochefoucauld, if not any longer Protestant, were associated with the more individualistic pieties of Jansenism; but many things are unclear.

We can more easily imagine the rooms these people had. The decorative style in the seventeenth century was still more or less sumptuous, and more or less Italianate, with carved wood-paneled walls, sometimes painted, and dark wooden furniture in the style we associate with the Three Musketeers, or Romeo and Juliet: velvet or brocade upholstery, fringes, square-seated chairs with spiral-turned legs. This decor would give way in the eighteenth century to lighter woods, chairs upholstered in silk brocades, pastels and gilding—the style we associate with Louis XV.

Sometimes I dare to go into the antiques shops around the corner on the Quai Malaquais or the Quai Voltaire, just to look at the furniture and objets d'art being sold for ferocious prices. Though many now trade in the glamorous art deco furniture of the 1930s, eighteenth-century Louis XV and XVI (the default styles of the French aristocracy to this day) have their purveyors as well.

Whoever was living in our Paris apartment at the beginning of the eighteenth century (possibly Bernard Germain-Étienne de la Ville, Comte de Lacépède, the great eighteenth-century biologist) decided to update the decor, and had mirrors installed on all four walls of the salon in carved gold frames. In this way, the crystal chandelier is reflected in infinite regression in whichever direction you turn, and you see in the mirrors an immensely long corridor lit with dozens of chandeliers, a sort of metaphor for the Enlightenment, the mood during nearly a century, seemingly so civilized and wise, before the Deluge.

Mirrors, an Italian technology, were everywhere in Paris by the eighteenth century, a festival of glitter and glamour, reflecting fashionable beauties, everything was *doré,* gilded. People wore silk and began to powder their hair. The short rounded breeches, ruffled collars, and gartered stockings for men gave way to longer coats with deep cuffs and longer curls, and wavy wide-brimmed hats. The women wore wide skirts and higher necklines and decorous head coverings—hoods and lace caps with little trains down the back. What hadn't been built in St.-Germain-des-Prés in the seventeenth century was being built now—the handsome mint, the Hôtel de la Monnaie, for instance—so everything assumed very much the look it has today.

The Century of Voltaire

He who has not the spirit of his times has all their misery.
Voltaire, STANCES

If the seventeenth century had been La Rochefoucauld's, the eighteenth would be Voltaire's, the tone witty, acerbic, analytic, angry. The spate of Louises, from Louis XIII, who came to the throne in 1610, to Louis XVI, who fell in 1792, had dragged France into debt, corruption, and continued sectarian strife. Voltaire foresaw

> *the signs of a revolution which must infallibly come. I shall not have the pleasure of beholding it. The French reach everything late, but they do reach it at last. Young people are lucky. They will see great things. I shall not cease to preach tolerance upon the housetops until persecution is no more. The progress of the right is slow. The roots of prejudice are deep. I shall never see the fruits of my efforts, but their seeds must one day germinate.*

One wonders whether Voltaire would have survived the Revolution? Probably not; his mockery would have offended the earnest revolutionaries. On the other hand, his consummate cynicism may have directed him to a prudent escape. Would the Duc de La Rochefoucauld have survived? At any rate, in 1778 Voltaire died a natural death a few minutes' walk from here on what is now called the Quai Voltaire, only steps from where d'Artagnan had lived a century before him, and didn't live to see the revolution he had predicted.

Benefiting from the St.-Germain-des-Prés tradition of welcoming strangers, many of our famous American founders were here in Voltaire's day. Brian N. Morton, in his invaluable book *Americans in Paris,* tells about many of them: Benjamin Franklin, a great favorite with the French, lived in a hotel at 52 Rue Jacob, and, with John Jay and John Adams, signed the treaty recognizing American independence at number fifty-six; Thomas Paine, Jefferson, of course, and writers like Washington Irving (and later, James Baldwin) were also on Rue Jacob, and James Fenimore Cooper was nearby. Franklin and Voltaire were introduced to each other at a scientific meeting at the Louvre, and according to John Adams, stood awkwardly til the gathering crowd insisted they embrace in the French style; so they did, kissing each other's cheeks, neither quite knowing what he was supposed to say.

The American Revolution was behind them, and the French upheaval was still to come. I remember my surprise when I learned that the French today still view their revolution as glorious, despite all the gruesome things their ancestors did—leaving the last little Louis, Marie-Antoinette's boy, to starve and die alone in prison, for example, as if the guillotine executions weren't brutal enough. America does have some things on its conscience, but not as many things, at least until recently; it hasn't had time to run them up, though Guantanamo Bay will surely be mentioned by history, and Abu Ghraib, and the Japanese internment, too.

But even there, the Japanese citizens did not have their heads chopped off. (True, we had the Civil War; by now, which American, whether Yankee or Rebel, has not secretly wondered whether it might have been better to let the South secede? The two halves of our nation seem to feel so differently about everything.) But we aren't yet hardened to violence as a means of social change, or only as a last resort, while the French seem to believe that actual or symbolic violence is a necessary prelude to revolution, acted out each day in the endless numbers of demonstrators marching (cheerfully these days) every day about something—elementary school reform, gas and electrical workers' salaries, war—with festive banners and music. Is it paradoxical that with its origins in violence, theirs is a safe society and, even with our peaceful gradualism, ours is dangerous and gun-ridden?

There have been a number of bloody events in St.-Germain over the centuries, and the shadows lie over it still. It was near here, at the corner of Rue de Buci, where I shop for groceries, and what is now Boulevard St.-Germain, that Protestants Nicolas de Cène and Pierre Gavart had their tongues pulled out and were burned in 1557, dangling from a pillory so their limbs would be painfully charred before they were dead. (Louis XIII abolished this pillory in 1636.) It was around here that the Protestants were massacred on St.-Bartholomew's Day, still one of the most scurrilous events of French history, though there was apparently a huge gate at the Buci end of Rue Visconti, which, by someone's keeping it closed during the massacre, helped to save some of the residents of Rue Visconti. History doesn't record who it was who kept it closed. I have mentioned the massacre near the church of St.-Germain-des-Prés during the Revolution.

And it was nearby, in the Cour de Commerce St.-André, which lies at the St.-Germain end of the Rue de Buci, between St.-Germain and St.-André-des-Arts, that Dr. Guillotin experimented on sheep to perfect his instrument, at first called La Louisane, or Louisette. In the *cour,* also, the revolutionary Marat published his newspaper, *L'Ami du Peuple,* before meeting his fate at the hands of Charlotte Corday, who in turn would be executed at the guillotine. His house was torn down eventually, but photographs exist, for instance in Leonard Pitt's excellent *Promenades dans le Paris disparu.* And it was even nearer to home that the mob slaughtered sundry aristocrats and criminals being detained in the court of the prison of the abbey.

The Revolution, the Terror, are now bewildering, especially the way all the former colleagues turned on one another; one misstep and your friends would guillotine you the next day, the ultimate demonstration of the effects of political correctness. However, the most illustrious tenant of our apartment, Monsieur Lacépède, managed to keep his head; here he was, unscathed when it all ended. He had prudently left town during the Reign of Terror, when other prominent scientists, like Antoine Lavoisier, were beheaded without pity. Yet, with all the slaughter, life went on. Restaurant Le Procope, on the Rue de l'Ancienne-Comédie, which also gives into the Cour de Commerce, had been opened in 1686, was open during the Revolution, and thrives still.

PART TWO

ÉCOLE DES BEAUX-ARTS

The years that a woman deducts from her age are never lost.
They are added to other women's.

Diane de Poitiers

If you walk toward Boulevard St.-Germain on our side of Rue Bonaparte, in a few steps you come to the École des Beaux-Arts, the national graduate school of art and architecture. Behind a handsome grille you see a large courtyard with buildings on three sides. On the left, various architectural elements are preserved against the wall; on the right you'll see Queen Margot's church, Église des Petits-Augustins, with its facade taken from Anet, the château that belonged to Diane de Poitiers.

By the time of Queen Margot's birth in 1553, there had been a long tradition of powerful mistresses and female rulers in France—Queen Margot is only one of the remarkable women associated with this quarter. The constellation of names also leads back to an earlier century, the fifteenth century, to Diane de Poitiers.

Facade of the church of the École des Beaux-Arts

Standing in the courtyard of the École des Beaux-Arts, you feel that Diane de Poitiers is a personage at least as present as Queen Margot. This interesting lady, influential mistress of Queen Margot's father, Henri II, had as a young woman been at the court of Queen Margot's grandfather, François I. She was in fact twenty years older than her royal lover his son. Even before coming to France, I had always been fascinated with this namesake Diane, and, especially, would have liked to know the secrets of her unusually long career as femme fatale. (She was said to have bathed in milk, for one thing.)

Someone, possibly Queen Margot herself, commented about her father, that he "had all the faults of his father [François I], with a weaker mind," implying that France during her father's reign was really ruled by this "ancient mistress," who had wrested control of him from another, "the pious and learned Anne d'Étampes." Both these mistresses had to contend, of course, with Catherine de Médicis, the legal wife, but wife and mistress seemed not to have interfered with each other too much, at least during Henri II's lifetime. The minute he was dead, Catherine sent Diane back to her country place, where she died, at sixty-seven, of a fall from her horse. If you count Diane as a de facto queen, she is the fifth queen to be associated with this neighborhood, only by association with the facade of her château, as she really didn't live here. But she was in a way the fifth female ruler of France in this period, with Catherine and Marie de Médicis, Queen Margot, and Anne of Austria. (There have been not a few female military figures as well, including Joan of Arc, Duchesse de Montpensier, and Henri IV's mother, Jeanne d'Albret.)

There was also a long tradition for the courtesan—the word originally referred to members of the court rather than to kept women. Queen Margot tells of at least two episodes when her husband Henri fell in love with a lady of the court. One was a Madame de Sauves, one a woman referred to as "Fosseuse." Both times Henri fell in love at the same moment that the eye of the reigning king fell upon the same lady, so that the rivalry between Protestant Henri and Catholic Queen Margot's brothers played itself out in the bedroom as well as on the field of battle.

Henri IV was capable of good-natured behavior but more often got into a snit, as once when he thinks Queen Margot is not nice enough to his mistress Fosseuse when Fosseuse gets pregnant. Queen Margot, not having much choice, tries to be nice to this young woman, and offers to take her away to a remote spot during the last stages of her pregnancy, to quiet any scandal under the pretext of withdrawing to avoid an epidemic.

But Fosseuse refuses. "So far from showing any contrition, or returning thanks for my kindness," complains Margot, "she replied with the utmost arrogance." According to Margot, Fosseuse rants that:

> *she would prove all those to be liars who had reported {that she was pregnant by the King}, that, for my part, I had ceased for a long time to show her any marks of regard, and she saw that I was determined upon her ruin. These words she delivered in as loud a tone as mine had been mildly expressed; and, leaving me abruptly, she flew in a rage to the King my husband. He was very angry upon the occasion, and declared he would make them all liars who had laid such things to her charge. From that moment until the hour of her delivery, which was a few months after, he never spoke to me.*

One feels a little sorry for Fosseuse in this story, although she seems to have been somewhat undiplomatic. Because apparently one did not lightly say no to a king, and could only hope to gain some advantage from compliance.

Henri was a determined womanizer; Queen Margot recounts how one night he had some sort of fit, and lay for an hour in a coma:

*... occasioned, I supposed, by his excesses with
women, for I never knew anything of the kind to
happen to him before. However, as it was my
duty so to do, I attended him with so much care
and diligence that, when he recovered, he spoke of
it to everyone, declaring that, if I had not per-
ceived his indisposition and called for the help of
my women, he should not have survived the fit.*

In fact, it behooved Margot to have had a little char-
ity, given her own numerous lovers. But the point is
that the long-established conventions of sexual freedom
that have attracted not only the French, and not only
back then, were also attractive to our American forebears
and all the American travelers to Paris since then.

As I said, I feel a kind of affinity with Diane de Poitiers
on account of having her name. My friend Michelle, an
American married to a Frenchman, thinks that
American women who find themselves living in France
are apt to have been given Frenchified first names at
birth, as she was, and as was I. Maybe destiny steers the
Tammys and Wendys elsewhere. It was evidently some
Francophilia on the part of my parents that made them
think of this name, and spell it Diane in the French way,

not with the more English form, Diana. I came upon a list among my mother's papers of other names she and my father were considering, and these were also French: Charlotte, Margot, and Anne.

After Queen Margot's death in 1615, the new queen, Anne of Austria, continued the building of a church and convent for the Petits-Augustins—themselves an order of Augustinians called "petits" to distinguish them from the Grands Augustins, who had a convent of their own on the street of that name a few minutes away. Anne gave the credit to Margot for the finished church. The inscription on the chapel reads: "Le 21 Mars 1608, la Reine Marguerite, Duchesse de Valois, petite-fille du grand roi François, soeur de trois rois, et seule restée de la race des Valois, ayant été visitée et secourue de Dieu, comme Job et Jacob ... elle a bati et fondé ce Monastère."

Anne of Austria was the wife of Louis XIII, the monarch d'Artagnan faithfully served; her portrait hung in his rooms. By d'Artagnan's day, the little Chapel of Praises that had stood alone before then had been incorporated into the church of the Petits-Augustins we see today. Queen Anne's new church was a handsome, large structure that served the monks until the Revolution nearly two hundred years later and now sits within the precincts of the École des Beaux-Arts.

You enter the courtyard of the École des Beaux-Arts from Rue Bonaparte through gates topped with out-sized, almost postmodern-looking stone busts of Nicolas Poussin and Pierre Puget, two seventeenth-century painters, the former much admired today, the other more or less forgotten. The courtyard is itself a classé space, listed on the register of buildings that mustn't be altered or torn down. It is wide and cobbled, with a mythological figure—is she Art herself, or maybe France?—standing in the middle on her twenty-foot plinth, with archaeological morsels of pilasters and cornices stuck on the buildings to the right and left, and a handsome Palladian nineteenth-century building across the back, containing classrooms, the library, and an amphitheater where a giant mural pays homage to the great artists of history.

(Who was it who pointed out that in every frieze of great men across the face of an old building, some of the figures will be completely unfamiliar to modern eyes? And so it is with the pantheon of painters in the École des Beaux-Arts amphitheater mural, painted 1836–1841. Holbein le Jeune, certainly, but Arnolfo di Lapo? Vignole? Peruzzi? I have a lot of architectural history to learn. The immortalized figures are overwhelmingly French and Italian, of course. There is only one Englishman—Inigo Jones—and no American.)

At the time of the French Revolution, the revolutionaries had planned to destroy all vestiges of previous regimes, including the art, the calendar, and certainly the churches, and start over with a blank slate. It was an analogous situation, I suppose, to the looting that went on in Iraq in 2003, the difference being that the French *revolutionaires* had more things to loot. Many a French family still preserves the finger bone of a king, the scrap of a bonnet, motley souvenirs of that time, handed down with increasing vagueness as to the provenance, and increased carelessness in dusting. Religious buildings were deconsecrated, and many were despoiled or destroyed completely, but somehow an enterprising archaeologist, Alexandre Lenoir, was allowed to commandeer the Église des Petits-Augustins for a museum. He was given the power to gather together various parts of discarded and destroyed tombs, statuary, and pieces of torn-down buildings into a museum of monuments, thus luckily preserving much of French heritage that would otherwise have been smashed to bits.

I had been looking at the church in the École des Beaux-Arts complex for six months before I was ever able to go inside, for it is usually closed now, except for the exhibitions, or *expositions,* as the French call them, but it is worth trying to see inside if it is open. (It is always possible on the guided visit on Monday afternoons, by appointment; to reserve call 01 47 03 50 74.) Even if it isn't, you'll see the facade, taken from Diane de Poitiers's château, her initials entwined with those of Queen Margot's father Henri II. (At Blois, the appearance of this monogram, entwined *H*'s and *D,* is explained as denoting "Henri Deux.") To see the chapel, you have to go inside the church, or else look out of my kitchen window. But the church itself, the courtyard, the facade of Diane de Poitiers's château—all these are visible from Rue Bonaparte.

The facade of Anet is worldy in its origins and also its details—statues of the pagan goddess Diana the huntress, classical columns, the initials celebrating earthly pomp, and so on. Anet was begun in 1548 by Henri II's architect Philibert de l'Orme, and worked on by sculptors Jean Goujon and Jean Cousin, and, less certainly, Benevenuto Cellini. It, too, was slated for destruction when Alexandre Lenoir saved it and brought it to Paris. The rest of the château still exists and can be visited. It was Lenoir who added statues of Apollo and Diana in the niches about half way up.

The wooden doors from Anet are particularly beautiful, decorated with Diane de Poitiers's monogram—two *D*'s facing each other, their backs forming the sides of an *H* for Henri. Later in her life Diane would add stags, antlers, and the moon to her personal iconography. As she still seems a vivid presence, it's interesting to keep in perspective that she was born more than five hundred years ago, in 1499, only seven years after Columbus sailed for America. And it is odd that although Columbus seems a figure of distant antiquity, Diane de Poitiers is intimately present.

Apropos of Diane, recently I went with a friend to the town of Étampes, a place an hour outside Paris where no one goes. Étampes was a French royal retreat in the fifteenth and sixteenth centuries, on the banks of the Juine and Chalouette Rivers—now home of a watercress festival and nothing much else to be said for it except for an amazing, ruined, round tower, of the sort the French call a *donjon,* all that is left of an ancient palace. This is the "Prison of Ingeburge," standing on a rampart above the village, where, apparently, various minorities—Africans and North Africans—have now come to live, but where kings did live. The dungeon tower was built in the thirteenth century by Philippe-Auguste, whose great wall surrounding Paris is now to be seen in a few places, including the parking garage on the Rue Mazarine which I have mentioned.

My friend was writing a piece for the travel section of the *New York Times* on the nearby famous garden of Méréville, and I had gone along for the lunch; we had planned to check out a local inn where *Times* readers might perhaps be guided to eat. On the main street we stopped before the local library, a locked and shut but ancient-looking place that said in tiny letters on its sign that it was a classified building *"dit de Diane de Poitiers,"* Duchess of Étampes. As we were wondering how to get in, a man came along, like a figure in a fairy tale, and offered to open the large wooden doors of the gate with a key from his big bunch of keys.

We went into the graveled courtyard. Across it was a lovely and old, rather touchingly small sixteenth-century building—noble houses would become larger and more grandiose in the seventeenth century. This one was of two stories, with stone carvings by the ubiquitous Jean Goujon around the door and on the gables and a mossy slate roof. Inside, something of a letdown, a cheerful modern library, with the banal lowered ceiling of perforated soundproofing tiles and rack of bulletins and announcements, and the New Book shelf standard in all libraries. The librarian stepped out to talk to us—she was closed for lunch. On the door and amid the carvings, the same two *D*'s forming an *H* that we see on the Anet facade, also worked on by Jean Goujon. Just tracking the works of a prolific sixteenth-century sculptor like Goujon gives a good idea of what the life of a prosperous artisan/artist was like then, itinerant and varied. Goujon worked on the Louvre, at Anet, and on many other famous châteaux, and did numberless statues, but would die in Italy, in exile for his Huguenot beliefs.

To return to the contents of the Église des Petits-Augustins in the École des Beaux-Arts: Lenoir's museum, established after the Revolution, would stay a museum until the restoration of the monarchy in 1814, when some of the bits were given back to those who had possessed them originally but had lost them in the upheavals, happy to have kept their heads. Like kings, religion had come into fashion again, the churches were reconstituted, and the monuments were moved to other sites or restored to the families and churches they had belonged to. This period of restitution decimated Lenoir's collection, though luckily many things made their way to the Louvre—for instance, Diane de Poitiers's fountain, a lush work begun by some unknown sculptor for her Anet château and finished by Pierre-Nicolas Beauvallet in 1799–1800, showing the naked goddess Diana and a stag reclining on an urn.

The next phase for the church/museum was as a fine arts college, the École des Beaux-Arts. This institution took over the whole complex of the Petits-Augustins, cloister and courtyard, in 1832 to harbor copies or *moulages* of great artworks, taken mostly from the Italian and meant for the training of art students who might not be able to go to Italy to see these mighty works for themselves. Copies of great statues were gathered to inspire them, and to form part of their course of study.

If you have a chance to go in, do. (I have mentioned that this can be arranged in advance.) Inside you will see a hangar-size, barrel-vaulted space, ceiling painted blue, whose oxblood walls are decorated by copies of famous paintings from Carpaccio to Ghirlandaio, and dominated by a vast rear wall showing the Last Judgment, copied from the Sistine Chapel.

To the right you can enter Queen Margot's chapel, which has numerous copies of famous sculpture: Michelangelo's works—the "Pietà," "Prisoners," the Médicis's tombs, slightly reduced in scale—and others, like the Ghiberti doors and some of the famous French royal tombs. These copies seem neglected, blackened and chipped, quite unlike the gleaming marble one sees in Italy; disappointing until it occurred to me that the copies date from a time when the Italian statues and paintings were probably dark with age and pollution, and the copyist had faithfully reproduced the patina he saw. Similarly, the "Last Judgment" is as it would have been seen a hundred years ago, before the recent cleaning of the work in Rome, lending to these copies a kind of historical interest of their own. The artist Xavier Sigalon, dispatched to Rome to make copies of some of the paintings when more influential painters thought it would be a waste of their talent, was fated to die there of cholera soon after finishing his work.

Beside housing the rather dusty and pocked plaster copies, the museum now also serves as a temporary gallery space, most recently showing drawings by the American artist David Smith, whose chaste abstractions were in striking contrast to the baroque ornaments ranged around the dim interior, and, this week, some drawings by the original architect of the École, Felix Duban (1798–1870), who designed the rest of the grand early nineteenth-century buildings in the courtyard.

THE ARCH

*{The church was} originally lit by high arched windows
(traces of which can still be seen from the outside).*

THE SIXTH ARRONDISSEMENT:
A GUIDE TO ITS HISTORY AND ARCHITECTURE

For awhile, a mystery remained, outside our kitchen
window, about the bricked-up arch in the wall the
chapel (and my kitchen) are attached to. One of the
great torments of my life was the wish to know what
that archway was or what it once led to. I asked
Emmanuel Schwartz, the librarian of the École des
Beaux-Arts, whose book on the chapel has been fascinating and useful; he knows all about the chapel, but he
couldn't explain about the arch, no doubt because my
description was so imperfect. I had not yet realized that
the arched wall ran along to become my kitchen wall.

At first I wondered if it were a part of some ancient
wall enclosing Paris? I went to check again the vestige of
the wall of Philippe-Auguste that remains in the parking

garage on the Rue Mazarine, a few minutes' walk from Rue Bonaparte. I was fairly sure that my wall was not a part of that ancient wall, built to defend the Paris of 1200; old maps and drawings show the wall of Philippe-Auguste a little to the east. But I wanted to look again, to see if there was any resemblance that might indicate a date for mine; so I descended into the parking lot on Rue Mazarine, as if I was looking for my car.

Most people are interested in archaeology whatever is dug up. In California, when we remodeled our 1906 house on Telegraph Hill in San Francisco, the workmen unearthed old whiskey bottles, the bones of two cats, and a shoe. I kept the old bottles. Bottles seem to survive everywhere, strangely resilient testimonials to the habits of vanished times; and in the Louvre one can see old bottles from around here, shimmering little things of glass dating from the Roman beginnings, dug up in the course of some repairs to the Louvre or Notre-Dame cathedral.

My wall makes me marvel at the way the French have built on history—that is, using it concretely, recycling the bricks and mortar and stones, to found the new. Buildings, like the Musée de Cluny, are sometimes built over Roman beginnings and the vestiges of medieval ditches influence the modern names. We have seen that, at the north side of the church of St.-Germain-des-Prés, remnants of things that were torn out of it during the

Revolution are affixed to its sides. The physical disman-
tling of so many monuments and buildings vandalized
during the Revolution (to say nothing of melting down
the statues and scattering the bones of their kings)
seems in contrast to, say, the Russians who during their
revolution tended to preserve the artifacts of the tsars,
their art and palaces, the contents of museums, and so
on. Of course, the Russian Revolution was later by more
than a century, and people's attitudes must have evolved
everywhere, though to say that is immediately to remember the Taliban blowing up the Buddhas.

As I mentioned, the French also seem to believe, at
least by tradition, that violence, even if symbolic, like the
otherwise lame, traffic-blocking little *manifestations,* or
manifs, that disrupt the streets of our quartier all the time,
are a necessary precondition for social change—in contrast to our society, otherwise so much more violent but
where political violence is rare. (Europeans could not
understand why we were not in the streets after the
election of 2000.) One day near here, on the corner of the
Rue du Bac and the Boulevard St.-Germain, I saw a fresh
puddle of blood where plumbers, or maybe schoolteach-
ers, had been marching, and someone had been wounded.

Sometimes, respect for the archaeology of Paris sets up
unexpected conflicts, though people don't take to the
streets about it. A few months ago, workers digging

around the Orangerie—the building at the west end of the Tuileries fronting the Place de la Concorde—came upon a wall constructed in the sixteenth century by Charles IX, and then continued by Henri III, two of the three brothers of Queen Margot, and eventually covered over by Le Nôtre, the garden designer for Louis XIV. Now the modern French authorities have to decide what to do with their discovery, and the place is closed until 2006.

This wall has engendered the predictable standoff between those who want to save it, which would mean changing or putting on hold the projected enlargement of the Orangerie museum, which presently contains, among other things, an installation of *Nymphéas,* the beautiful, rather absent-minded water-lily paintings of Monet, and others, including the state, who want to demolish the relatively ordinary-looking pile of stones. A commission of architects and archaeologists has been studying the possibilities, and the government has come in for reproaches for not having foreseen that they would probably dig up something precious in such a sensitive location. The guess is it will probably opt for a way of incorporating the wall into its museum-enlargement scheme, and, meantime, a public subscription has been announced for rebuilding the Tuileries palace from scratch, which the people burned in 1871 during the Commune, that peculiar and short-lived uprising that people would think back on fearfully during the social upheavals of May 1968.

If the Tuileries are rebuilt, it will restore a structure built by Catherine de Médicis but abandoned out of superstition. Queen Margot tells of her mother's belief in omens and predictions: "Many have held that God has great personages more immediately under his protection, and that minds of superior excellence have bestowed on them a good genius, or secret intelligence, to apprise them of good, or warn them against evil," she wrote, this view contrasting with more politically correct modern views that God cares as much for the peasant as for the prince. "Of this number I might reckon the Queen my mother, who has had frequent intimations of the kind; particularly the very night before the tournament which proved so fatal to the King my father; she dreamed that she saw him wounded in the eye, as it really happened."

She makes no claims for herself: "I am far from supposing that I myself am worthy of these divine admonitions," yet she herself has had warnings, belying her modest denial; she goes on to recount how she was once struck by a bizarre shivering fit when she encountered one of her brothers, Henri, who was plotting against her, and was himself the victim of intriguers who were trying to turn him against her, because she was loyal to another brother and was married to Henri of Navarre.

In the case of the abandoned Tuileries palace, Catherine was told she would die "near to St.-Germain," which she thought referred to the palace itself, but the prophecy turned out instead to refer to the priest named St.-Germain who gave her the last rites twenty-two years later. The Tuileries Palace was eventually finished by Henri IV, used by all the Louises to a greater or lesser extent, and by Napoleons I and III, and then, as we have seen, burned down.

I have a friend, Sally W., who lives at 12 Rue Bonaparte. Looking at our building from Sally's third-floor apartment gave me some new perspective on our filled-in arch. From her window, I could see along the walls of the church up to the place where the chapel protrudes, and now I could see that the wall outside my window, its arch filled in but the outlines still visible, is a wall of the church of the Petits-Augustins in the Beaux-Arts complex. That is, my kitchen is built smack up against the church, in a sense is actually a part of it; this suggests that my kitchen dates from an earlier era than the rest of our apartment, and was part of a convent built onto the church.

But what was the arch? From some old engravings that a friend has found, it appears to have been a window of the church that has been filled in, leaving the outline of the arch in place. One of the engravings shows the church to have had just these arched windows in the days of Anne of Austria. I have also found a French guidebook about the sixth arrondissement that confirms that the church used to have high arched windows, subsequently bricked up, "traces of which can still be seen from the outside" and, finally, there are paintings in the Musée Carnavalet, the museum of the city of Paris, showing the interior of the Église des Petits-Augustins in Lenoir's time, with light shining though arched windows that are today no longer visible inside. So it appears that the simple explanation is that the arch was a window, now filled in.

Speaking of windows, one of the most charming customs of local architecture is that of painting a trompe l'oeil window if the eye expects a window that is in fact bricked up. Sometimes the passerby doesn't even notice the false one among the real. A good example is at the southwest corner of Rue St.-Sulpice and Rue de Condé, as you are looking south from Boulevard St.-Germain.

All over Paris, bits of old or former Paris are used as part of the new, but there are many parts of the city where the new is not allowed to show on the outside. Facades are preserved and the interiors, unless they are classé, can be rebuilt behind them. A few days ago I wandered into 12 Rue des Sts.-Pères, where the doors stood open and tarps and scaffolding lay about, indicating a remodeling project. A sign, evidently intended for some delivery man, said to go up to the first floor, so I did, up the magnificent staircase.

I seemed to remember that there had been a developer's sign on this building a few months earlier, calling it the Hôtel de Noailles, referring to the famous family of aristocrats who apparently had some association with this location. Their most famous house, in the Place des États-Unis, has recently been bought by Baccarat, remodeled by Philippe Starck, and displays sumptuously the collection of fine glassware assembled by this famous company of glassmakers, preserving some of the Noailles's decor behind new wall coverings painted by the contemporary artist Gérard Garouste.

Inside the Sts.-Pères building, the site was humming with restorers, people sanding and pounding. Certain architectural elements had recognizably been retained— the shutters of the windows, some of the parquet, carefully covered in tarp. In other places, new underflooring had been laid. Bare wires dangled from ceilings—there were no moldings or ceiling rosettes, but maybe these would come back. The height of the ceilings was magnificent, the light through the long windows superb; yes, somebody had bought it, the contractor said. All the apartments in this building had been sold at enormous prices. This one was in the millions of euros, though he would not say how many or whose, or how much it was costing to restore it to its seventeenth-century magnificence.

Académie Française

A serious man has few ideas; a man of ideas is never serious.
Paul Valéry, Mauvaises Pensées et Autres

I am a housewife and a novelist, two activities that don't really fit together, in that I find it too easy to skip working at my writing in the name of (mostly undone) things that need doing around the house. The solution is to get out of the house and work somewhere else, and in my case, I go to the Bibliothèque Mazarine, the library inside the Institut de France. Instead of walking south on Bonaparte to St.-Germain, which takes me by the École des Beaux-Arts, I instead turn left, walk toward the Seine, turn right at the corner of Bonaparte and the Quai Malaquais, and walk another minute or two along the quay to the Institut de France, the grand building that dominates the Quai Malaquais where it turns into the Quai de Conti.

The ensemble of the Institut de France was designed by the genius Louis Le Vau, Louis XIV's architect for

Quai Malaquais

Versailles, the Louvre, and various great châteaux. D'Artagnan would have seen the Institut more or less in its present form, just as he would have seen the nearby Hôtel de la Monnaie, the beautiful, immense eighteenth-century neoclassic structure built onto a house that was started in the thirteenth century, remodeled in 1572, 1641, and 1670, and became the national mint in 1768 under Louis XV—a great example of the evolution of buildings with their times. Today the money-coining facility itself has moved, but decorative coins and medals are still made here, and it is worth stopping in to see the beautiful staircase and interesting museum.

The Bibliothèque Mazarine is open to all for a small yearly fee and a look of seriousness, or maybe looking serious is not required. When I first went to the Flore to meet Monsieur B., someone said by a mutual friend to be (and is) incredibly knowledgeable about the "inner" St.-Germain, I asked him "How will I recognize you?" He said, "I look like a *clochard*," which is in our parlance a homeless person and maybe a drunk. (Of course he is neither a drunk nor a homeless person, I should hasten to add.) Nonetheless, Monsieur B. has a library card to the Mazarine, the first public library in France, founded by Cardinal Mazarin in 1648—a library open to all. While I'm not sure whether a clochard could get a card at the San Francisco Public Library, the point is they are welcome at the Bibliothèque Mazarine.

In the Bibliothèque Mazarine, the student can write or read in undisturbed splendor, and here I work, though this magnificent library is almost too grand, with its sixty-five-foot ceilings, great gilt chandeliers, leather-topped tables (nicely wired for the computer), and welcoming but always impassive librarians. I have yet to summon the nerve to ask for a book, but I do sidle along the shelves, eyeing the massive leather-bound volumes and occasionally consulting the dictionaries. Also, there is still a card catalog, a joy to leaf through, the oldest entries handwritten in the seventeenth century. The librarians here have had the wisdom to keep it, unlike American libraries which have mostly dispensed with or even destroyed their card catalogs—without knowing, as they will admit, how long electronic data can be expected to last. (I've always admired Nicholson Baker's diatribes on this subject.) There is also an array of French literary and historical periodicals, perfect for browsing and putting off the daily confrontation with a manuscript in progress.

I went there almost every day to work on my novel *L'Affaire,* aware that the librarians must have thought I was also some sort of stray, a homeless person sheltering from the cold, a token piece of paper in front of me, toying with a pen, staring into air. I gained a couple of pounds, too, from each day buying a chocolate *rocher* at the Tabac des Beaux-Arts at my corner to nibble surreptitiously instead of going home to lunch. Another means of procrastination is to walk slowly around the vast *salle* of the reading room, inspecting the parade of marble busts of Cicero, Homer, Condorcet, and other ancients that line the aisles, their sage countenances seeming to impart brotherly encouragement, as it seems on the days when all is going well, or else a certain scorn for mere modern literary toil, fiction at that, when it isn't.

The beautiful Institut de France, at first called the Collège des Quatre-Nations, was founded in 1661 by provisions in the will of Cardinal Mazarin, finished in 1672, opened in 1688. If you face it with your back to the river, you see a wide forecourt with a gilded, domed chapel, which, with Queen Margot's Chapel of Praises, was one of the first domes in Paris—the technology coming from Italy in the tradition of Brunelleschi or Michelangelo. The chapel is flanked by two curved wings. The Mazarine Library faces the Seine in the left wing of this imposing building, which also houses the Académie Française and other French institutions, with a lecture hall in the chapel at the center. This chapel is normally closed—I have only seen inside it once, on the day in September when all French public buildings, many in historic palaces and *hôtels particuliers,* are thrown open for the public, and French people line up to inspect these valuable instances of their *patrimoine,* the collective patrimony they all appreciate—but only the public servants get to use on a daily basis.

It's here that the *immortels* are inducted into the Académie Française, the august assembly of men of letters, with once in a while a woman. It isn't given to Americans, usually, to meet members of that distinguished group, but by accident I have met one, not through literary channels but because of that apartment-hunting propensity I have mentioned. I was helping Carolyn Kizer, the distinguished, Pulitzer

Prize–winning American poet and fellow Californian, and her husband, John Woodbridge, the architect (who has written a marvelous *Guide to Paris),* look for an apartment. Arthur Hall Smith, an American painter now living in Paris, was the fourth of our party.

We were a bit late for a rendezvous with the real estate agent, and he/she had gone, leaving us standing in confusion in the foyer of an elegant seventeenth-century building discussing what to do next. At the same time, a pizza deliverer came in, rang, and we saw a beautiful woman in her housecoat who had been waiting for him upstairs and had overheard us. She accepted the pizza, then said to us, in perfect but rather oddly idiomatic English, "I'm sorry the guy is gone, but if you'd like to see an apartment in this building, you can have a look at ours, they are all somewhat like this." (The French all use the word "guy," clearly an artifact of correct English lessons of a while ago; we do say it, but, unlike this woman, most never seem to use it in quite the right context, a great warning never to use the slang of a language not your own.)

It seemed rude to refuse, even though it was evident that she lived in a large, splendid place and our lot, as Americans in Paris, is usually to inhabit the unwanted first floors and mezzanines; Carolyn and John weren't planning to buy a sumptuous whole upper floor on the Rue Guénégaud, but we went in.

"I'm sorry, my husband isn't home," she said. "This is his day for the Academy." Now we were thrown into a bit of a panic. Académie Française?! Whose house were we in? We looked around with extra penetration, as she led us through several splendid rooms into his beautiful and imposing library. We squinted at the framed photos on the tables and tried to read the titles of the books in the shelves. Finally, brilliant Arthur, spying a familiar title, had a brainstorm: "Not Jean Dutourd! *Le Bon Beurre?*" he asked.

"Yes!" And she was Madame Dutourd, Camille.

The rest of us were struck dumb with embarrassment. I, at least, had no clue as to who that was, and apparently Carolyn and John were in the same boat. Now that I've read a number of his novels, I know that Jean Dutourd is my favorite French writer, as well as the best one going (an unfashionable opinion that shocks my French friends, for he is, by lefty French lights, conservative), and maybe the only one to have plot and humor that anglophones can understand (I don't rule out they may have humor we don't understand). *The Horrors of Love* is my favorite, a masterpiece. Any novelist will be struck dumb with admiration for this highly amusing tour de force: a seven-hundred-page novel consisting of a dialogue between two friends strolling through Paris, discussing the love life and fate of a politician friend of theirs, recently in prison. Not one second of it boring. Oddly enough, *Le Bon Beurre,* which made him famous, is the only one of his novels I haven't been able to find in English. I like his writing so much, I don't want to risk reading it in French, because I want to really enjoy it. I've been reading in French a long time, but only occasionally find a book engrossing enough that I lose the sense of reading in a foreign language; that is, of not somehow receiving the sense of the words indirectly, like wading in socks.

Le Bon Beurre, about black marketeers during the Second World War, I have read described by someone as eminent as V. S. Pritchett (perhaps it was he?) as the greatest Second World War novel in French, or perhaps the greatest, period. All Dutourd's work is witty and worldly as well as wise—a tone that modern French writing rarely seems to find. To our taste much of it is rather *"Oh! Stupeur!"* in the declamatory style the French appear to admire, a manner that to us amounts to "fine writing," the sin people writing in English are taught to avoid.

The story goes on. Carolyn, with her characteristic good nature and generosity, thinking over this episode next day, said, "There's something not right here. Why was that woman in her housedress at three in the afternoon? I think she's depressed, and especially when he goes off to his clubby little lunches. Let's invite her to lunch ourselves."

We did; she declined, did not ever go out to lunch, but instead said that she and her husband had decided that they would like us all to meet them for dinner one night at Brasserie Lipp, the venerable institution on Boulevard St.-Germain. We were shown to the best table—I've learned that there are bad and good tables at Lipp, which practically rules out going there without a French friend, for fear of getting a bad one, almost an inevitability to someone with an American accent and an unknown face. Also, the food isn't exceptional, and there are no rules against cigars.

But, sitting at a privileged table, one has the chance to gape at the other regulars. That night, at the next table was Maurice Herzog, the great climber of Annapurna. That feat was in 1950, but he still looks fit and attractive, except, of course, no tips of fingers. His book about the expedition, called, I think, *Annapurna,* recounts how he lost them to frostbite.

Anyway, the dinner. Jean Dutourd was affability itself to this rabble his wife had somehow collected. At one juncture I asked him if they often invited a pack of strange Americans to dinner? "Never," he said. "This is the first time. But after this, I'll make a point of doing so." That chivalrous reply is very French, or at least very Jean Dutourd.

We remained in touch, and would all get together whenever the Woodbridges came to stay in the pied-à-terre they eventually found. I've been struck at how the waiters, in whatever restaurant we go to, recognize a French academician and are powerfully impressed and extra gracious, and I couldn't help but reflect that, for better or worse, writers in America, except for a few, are not fawned over by waiters, or even noticed. Of course, I also noticed that the Dutourds were HUGE tippers—*noblesse oblige,* I suppose. Upon leaving the restaurant, Camille gave a clochard a hundred francs. "It's just for drink," she told the man, and that seems very French too, if, in our parlance, "enabling." It's our puritanism, the French would say, that keeps us from enabling a drunk; it's true, I would have been disapproving of that man spending his windfall on drink instead of something nutritious.

Jean Dutourd is or was on a committee of the Académie Française that is revising the French dictionary. Unlike English, French has, or would like to have, a fixed vocabulary, and vigilantly guards against incorporating new words from foreign languages. But of course it does add them, and then the academicians have to rule them in or out. Some words, like "weekend," are invincible; others are weaker, like "seat belt," and can be repulsed. I believe he told me they work in the mornings, then go to lunch; and sure enough, one day when I was lunching at Le Cafetière on the Rue Mazarine, I was told that the academicians were upstairs, very jolly after their labors. When these august, and mostly elderly, gentlemen came downstairs, they did look quite flushed and cheerful. There have been a couple of women in the Academy—Marguerite Yourcenar was the first—but probably not on that committee.

Some Neighbors

Vieille maison, Lacépède y vivait en 1801.
Guide Practique

Our kittens, Babbage and Watson, love to prowl in the inner court outside our kitchen window in the shadow of the Chapel of Praises. This little court, perhaps twenty by thirty feet in size, is bisected by a low wall that separates the space between our building and number ten, the building next door. It is planted with pots of ivy and hedge and flowers, and gives an experience of the natural world to their cloistered lives. Luckily, there's nowhere they can escape out of it, though Babbage once climbed precariously to a rain gutter that rims the chapel and had to be rescued by ladder.

The garden is tended by a woman, a passionate gardener. She introduced herself as *La Voisine*—the neighbor. I don't know her name, though perhaps she mentioned it. La Voisine and I speak in French, which limits me, but when our friends Fran and Bu come to spend the summer in our apartment, they talk to her, and Fran reports that La Voisine speaks English perfectly well. Most people around here speak English perfectly well; Americans used to complain that they didn't, but now the disappointing thing is that they do, and insist on it whenever they detect an American accent. Not La Voisine, however. She politely sticks to the language we spoke at the beginning.

(This reminds me of a pet peeve—when French waiters, hearing your American accent, change into English and refuse to speak French, even if you, always hoping to practice and improve, resolutely stick to French. Almost worse is the menu in English, with its inevitably bizarre translations, so that you have to ask for a menu in French to find out what you'll be eating.)

The chapel wall forms one of the limits of La Voisine's space. On its other three sides are her doorway, the half wall that she sets her plants along, and the high stone surface with the ancient bricked-up archway in it that forms the back wall of the Église des Petits-Augustins and runs along to become the back wall of my kitchen. La Voisine has valiantly painted the lower part of the chapel wall white, probably in violation of the architectural protections legislating the exterior treatment of historic buildings in this neighborhood, but in an inner court, who is to see or report? Our conversations concern her gardening, which requires her to climb over the low wall to pose her pots and trellises on our side, and, now, the kittens. She loves cats, she says, but is apprehensive for her plants. I foresee that we will eventually have to replace some of them, but so far the kittens, joyful to be outside, tiptoe among the pots with utmost delicacy.

I don't garden, because the floor of my side of the court is a skylight for the underground storage area of an art gallery in our building. This storage area in our basement, or *cave,* is linked, I am told, by a series of underground passages all the way to the church of St.-Germain-des-Prés. There is also a frightening, deep well, perhaps a vestige of the branch of the Seine which trickled along Rue de Petite-Seine, one of the names of our street before it became Bonaparte. Or it might be a *source,* or spring—no one knows, but they are sure that it provided water for the monks of the convent of the Petits-Augustins.

Two retired neighbors have done some research on such archaeological aspects of the neighborhood—a military man and an *avocat,* or lawyer, both of whom have interested themselves in the history of Rue Bonaparte buildings. (One must be called *maître,* for that is what lawyers are called, and the other *mon colonel,* by men though not by women.) Luckily, we have moved to a first-name basis. Jean-Jacques and Robert. (Perhaps they accede to this American familiarity because they know our louche ways.)

Jean-Jacques and Robert say that the caves communicate via passages and troughs with those of the church of St.-Germain-des-Prés, but for the moment I find them too creepy to explore. I would, however, like to see an inscription said to have been scratched on the wall of a cave at number twelve Bonaparte by Huguenots hiding there, something told me by a noted American composer, but unconfirmed by Jean-Jacques, who hasn't yet taken me down there.

As we found, hunting for real estate in Paris is one way of getting to see places you might never otherwise get inside. Curiosity is part of the reason we happened on our apartment. John and I were seriously in the market for a bigger apartment, but John is not much for idle browsing. Luckily, my friend Bob and I are, so it was Bob and I who went with Monsieur Chevallier, the real estate agent, to have a look at something he proposed. It was a gloomy day in December, and a nondescript building, but close to the Seine, where I love being. We climbed the stairs to find sinister developers standing in the foyer of the apartment discussing putting in a mezzanine under the tall ceilings, ripping out the boiserie of the living room, and dividing the place into two apartments—animating our anxiety at the mere idea of changes to this more or less unchanged and lovely space, however shabby, and all painted a bubblegum pink. "You have to have it," Bob said. As he used to be my editor, I obey him in all things.

Of course, like everything, the apartment cost more than we had planned to spend or thought we could, but I hoped that love would find a way, and luckily, when John was brought round to see it, he fell in love, too. Despite the primitive bathroom with its pull-chain toilet, and the phone extensions strung on overhead wires, bob-and-spool wiring, and other vestiges of resistance to the modern world, we began to have long conversations about how we could make it work. We were glad nothing much had been done to the place since, in the nineteenth century, someone had lowered the ceiling in the hall to construct a little overhead room for a servant, who had to climb to her bed up tiny, nearly vertical stairs.

I keep repeating the basic question that nobody can answer for sure—when was our building built? I put this question out among my friends and people I thought would likely know. My two best-informed neighbors have no answers for sure, and *"Vieille maison. Lacépède lived here in 1801,"* is all I can learn from either the *Guide Practique* or Hillairet's *Dictionnaire.*

"Part of the seventeenth-century convent," said Mme. D., on the third floor, our upstairs neighbor, to whose family our building has belonged since an ancestor bought it right after the Revolution. Her father agreed with this date. James Ivory, the director, who lives a block away and is very knowledgeable about Parisian architecture because of films he has made here, believes it to be "middle 1700s," on the basis of his building at the corner of Rue Jacob, part of which is eighteenth century, part—the part where an American designer, Vicky Tiel, has her workroom—seventeenth century or even earlier. She has been forbidden by the Ville de Paris from altering her space consecrated to alterations.

"Our building is 1629," sniffed my neighbor Drusilla. She's at number six, next to us, and in fact attached to us via a little building in the courtyard. Finally, a sort of consensus holds that some of our building was built in the seventeenth century, originally part of the convent built by Queen Margot and then Anne of Austria for the Petits-Augustinians, then added to in the eighteenth century, and a story added—the building is four stories high now. Many of the seventeenth-century buildings got an extra story later, either in the eighteenth or nineteenth centuries, when people built onto the roofs.

Other neighbors come forth with other historical details. Madame de M., across the street, with her adorable dog, says that the windows of her apartment were blocked up at the kitchen level by the seventeenth-century Marquis de Persan, who planned to rent it out but was suddenly afraid his tenants would toss their *déchets* and *ordures* into his courtyard. Garbage, that is. Accounts of the filth of early Paris are pretty harrowing, and sewage flowed in the street.

When confronted with the name of the Marquis de Persan, I suddenly realized that is almost the name of one of the characters in my novels about Paris, Antoine de Persand, perhaps subliminally suggested, though I don't know where I could have come across it—perhaps in the invaluable Hillairet.

The Mysteries of French History

At number 3 bis, Lacordaire, Montelembert and Coux, who founded there the first École Libre in 1831 (inscription); at number 4, Pradier; at number 5, Gérard de Nerval; at number 13, Oscar Wilde, who died there in 1900; at number 10, Corot, Merimee and J.-J. Ampère; finally, at number 8, Fantin-Latour had his atelier in 1868.

Hillairet, Connaissance du Vieux Paris

A person raised and educated in America may have to start from scratch when it comes to French history, if I am any example. Who was Lacordaire? Who was Coux? The above passage describes a little section of the Rue des Beaux-Arts. Like Rue de l'Abbaye, Rue des Beaux-Arts leads between Rue Bonaparte and Rue de Seine, and had its share of celebrated and obscure inhabitants. Just walking on any street of St.-Germain with Hillairet's guide in hand makes me conscious of my almost complete ignorance of the events of French history, things that were unfolding, evidently, at the same time as things in England and, eventually, America, that form the focus of our anglo-oriented studies.

Until now, when I thought of the nineteenth century, I would think of Queen Victoria, but never of Louis-Philippe or Napoleon III. We do recognize a furniture style called Directoire, but the English term "Regency" is more familiar. I could never have enumerated the French kings before Louis XIII (then it gets simple up through Napoleon), but, like many who went to elementary school in America, I can do all the English kings beginning with William and even a few of the Saxons, plus Boadicea.

Walk over to the Rue de Seine via the Rue Visconti, and stop before, say, number twenty-four, which belonged, in 1599:

> to the poet Nicolas Vauquelin.... He became the teacher of César de Vendôme, then of the Dauphin in 1609; he left the court after the death of Henri IV, maybe disgraced by the boldness of his language. He then lived here a joyous epicurean, with a lady harp player, Jeanne Dupuy, picked up in the street.
>
> At the same number lived in 1658, the historian Nicolas Fontaine, who shared the work

and the hardships of the recluses of Port-Royal,
and was, at the Bastille from 1664 to 1669,
the companion in captivity of Lemaistre de Sacy.
In 1692 Racine lived here, for seven years until
he died ... in 1699.

The indefatigable Hillairet knew his French history, but which Californian knows who Vauquelin was, or Lemaistre de Sacy, or why the latter was in the Bastille? Thus is the neighborhood saturated with more history than I can recount, each building a place where hundreds of people have lived. It would take a lifetime to understand the history of every building of this quarter, and even then, what would we know of all that really happened, was felt, was regretted and celebrated? How can one recapture a sense of the life unfolding here?

Perhaps I'm extra fascinated by history because I myself come from a place with not much history at all, or not much by comparison, that I know of. The sole resonances of the past in Moline were the graves of Confederate soldiers who had been imprisoned in the Rock Island Arsenal and died there of something like yellow fever or smallpox. And then, a grandson of Charles Dickens, so it said on his tombstone, had strayed into our town—we never heard why—and was buried in the cemetery where we used to ride our bikes. Also, Mr. John Deere had set up his plow factory in Moline, but that was it for history.

Paris has been here for two thousand years. In some ways it is always new; in others it has a patina and a collective sensibility that probably took two thousand years to develop, though it is hard to pinpoint all the ways this is manifested. One way is its self-regard. Knowing itself to be a precious example of civilization, it is constantly taking care of itself, polishing, repairing, gilding, refacing. Buildings are obliged to have their faces washed every ten years. Buildings of stone must be sandblasted; buildings like ours, stuccoed over the stones, must be repainted, and very expensive it was, too, more than ten thousand euros just for John's and my share. The scaffolding eclipses the windows for weeks, and a scaffold is a signal to burglars that it is your turn for their attentions via the convenient means of entering you have provided.

The burglar who came to our building did reconnaissance first, disguised as a representative of the painting company. I thought it was odd that people doing the facade would want to look in our back bathrooms and kitchen, but I didn't tumble to his real game until another person in the building got suspicious, and called the police. Our burglar was gone in seconds, but weeks later, some false painters turned up, went into the apartment one floor above us, and began to help themselves. The building had to change all its locks, a project of immense expense and nuisance for everyone.

There are not so many of us in 8 Rue Bonaparte. This is a small building, with us on the first floor; the colonel and his wife on the second, and their two daughters each with her apartment and family on the second and third; a small pied-à-terre on the third floor, also owned by that family; and the art galleries on the street level. These are Mssrs. Marcel and David Fleiss, father and son, dealers in twentieth-century art, that is, early modernist and contemporary art; M. Felix Marcillac, who sells important art deco furniture; and Monsieur Rossignol, the bookseller. There is also a room for Errida, the *gardienne* (it is now considered non-p.c. to say "concierge"), who I think has to go into the entry of the cellar to shower. I have never wanted to know too much about this arrangement, but when I went down there with our late cat Walter who loved to prowl there, looking for cobwebs, I would sometimes hear a shower running. Until recently, the sanitary arrangements in many Parisian buildings involved a shared toilet on the landing, and God knows where the bath was; so I suppose Errida's situation is not entirely unusual. She is from Mexico, which is not common in Paris, and though, being Californian, I should speak a sort of Spanish, we speak to each other in our bad French.

It was the ancestor of the present family who bought our building after the Revolution, when all of Paris was for sale, and well-off middle-class people were able to buy real estate that had until then been the property of aristocrats and friends of the king—people who were beheaded. As I have mentioned, we are the sole outsiders in our building—otherwise all the apartments are lived in by three generations of the one family—grandparents, parents, and children, and there are even two great-grandchildren who are often brought to visit. Presumably some members of these three generations were themselves brought up in the building, just as their children are being brought up here now; there's also a country house where they all go on the (numerous) French vacations. I often think how nice this arrangement is, not unlike the communes idealistic Americans tried to form in the sixties (no doubt fraught with the same potential for squabbles).

There are so many advantages to this way of life. When one of the sisters happens to be out, the other can take in her packages or groceries; all the cousins grow up knowing each other, with babysitting always on hand; models of extended family life—so much nicer than the bleak isolation of an American suburb with the mothers going crazy, and rivers of gin. Of course, the French family may all detest each other, but they don't seem to, and if they do, they would never show it, with their good manners and unfailing charm.

We are not here in the summers, when, with the windows open, we could glean a better take on all the family relationships. In our last apartment, on Rue St.-Simon, it was a festival of Portuguese in the summers; all the gardiennes talking and gossiping and launching horrendous, audible quarrels.

To find the exact date of our building remains an unfulfilled quest.

DETAILS

Dorothy and I went on a walk. We only walked a few blocks but only in a few blocks we read all the historical names, like Coty and Cartier and I knew we were seeing something educational at last and our whole trip as not a failure.

Anita Loos, GENTLEMEN PREFER BLONDES
(quoted in Steven Barclay's A PLACE IN THE WORLD CALLED PARIS)

I am daunted by the elusive details of history, some of its figures to be discovered but none to be really heard or felt. What was the sound of their voices, what were the cooking smells in the corridor? My friend Mireille, who is a professor at the Sorbonne and an expert on the French language of the sixteenth century, says that it is known, at least, that Henri IV spoke French with a heavy Béarnais accent (though to me that only conjures tarragon and butter). She also tells me that even so late as the eighteenth century, even until the time of Voltaire, most French people didn't speak "proper" French, but some dialect like Provençal, or Catalan. The accents of people from the south of France still sound very Italian to me, with the same way of pronouncing *r,* the letter most dreaded by anglophones.

The Italian Catherine de Médicis spoke French but with a strong Italian accent, which was always disliked and criticized; and the strongest dislike was felt for some of her Italian courtiers—though not as strong as that felt for the Italian friends of Marie de Médicis, the greedy couple Concini. He was assassinated and she was burned as a witch. All these historical characters never to be heard, nor much known about their religion, their philosophies, or love lives! I have mentioned the odd reticence in modern reference books about religion. The early La Rochefoucaulds were Huguenots. I don't know about the many modern La Rochefoucaulds, including a woman who had an antique shop on the Rue de l'Université near here, and quite a few others—almost all countesses, as I confirm in my *Bottin Mondain,* a sort of social register of France. This is a fat book I once had the luck to find—someone had put it out on the street, outdated to be sure, but since things change slowly here, still very serviceable as a source of endless fascination and information. For instance, here is a sample passage chosen at random, with the names slightly altered by me in case the real people would mind: "Dubilliard (Guillaume) Colonel (ER) et Mme née Monique Pozac—10 rue

Dupine 44000 Mantes Tel 04 xxx, enfants Justine (du premier marriage du colonel avec Madame Nicole O'Haggerty), Brigitte (Mme Albert Godet), Flore-Annie (Mme Romulus Dupee), Roland, Henri."

What dramas are implied by the mention of the first marriage of the colonel and Mademoiselle O'Haggerty? The *Bottin* keeps nothing back. It also gives the floor plans of the various theaters and opera houses helpful for ordering tickets, and phone numbers of auctioneers. It is snobbish but democratic, so foreigners are admitted, as in the case of one Mme. Hervé Arzad, née Susan-Jane Moscovitz from Bronx, New York.

But the point is, even in the *Bottin* there seem to be no subtle clues (except, perhaps, having a Swiss medal), no reference to parish or temple, that would hint at their religious preferences, not important in the case of the modern Dubilliards, but for figuring out the social affinities of the *salonistes* or where someone stood in the Fronde, important. What was the religion of the author of the *Maxims?*

DETAILS:
Instead of lampposts on Rue Bonaparte and adjacent streets, the city of Paris has hung lanterns of the kind

they would have had in the eighteenth century, when the streets first began to be lighted. It is easy to forget how dark earlier nights must have been—gas lighting was only introduced on the public streets in 1829. Before that, various schemes had been tried—ordinances requiring everyone to put a candle in his window; mobile torch-carriers for hire who would see you home for a few coins. Rue Dauphine had oil lanterns for a time.

Running water, too, was a relatively modern invention. William Cole, in his Rue Bonaparte lodgings, had only a basin for handwashing. He doesn't mention other sanitary arrangements. Nor does Hillairet, beyond saying that Paris "was always a city *crotté*," meaning what one still notices on the sidewalks, now attributable to dogs, whose owners are enjoined to clean up after their pets, and some actually do.

The harmony of the facades is one of the things that gives Paris its exceptional beauty; the other is the fact that the buildings have been kept from going too high— six or seven stories is about the limit. The American architect John Field has a convincing theory about the livability of cities: that a height limit of around six stories (and a more dense habitation per square mile) should be the model for urban schemes in America— cities ought to fill in among existing buildings, not with high-rise but with buildings of this height, which allow for light, and visible sky, and a pedestrian's comfortable point of view. One proof that his theory produces an ideal urban environment is that Paris, without resorting to high-rises, has one of the highest population densities of cities anywhere, and apparently there is something innately compatible with human psyche about buildings of this height.

It is, anyhow, the formula the French are comfortable with and are keeping to inside Paris, though they have built some strange-looking high-rises outside the city. The present mayor of Paris has sounded a warning that high-rises inside the Périphérique (the ring road around the core city) were being studied, but he can probably expect a lot of public opposition, such as that which appeared with the Tour Montparnasse (in part blamed on an American developer), which most people felt spoiled the skyline, an eyesore that people avoid. (The mayor privately told a *New York Times* reporter he would like to tear it down.) Part of the Stalinist-looking medical school on the Rue des Sts.-Pères, built in 1937, so out of place among the beautiful seventeenth-century buildings, was torn down; the height was reduced by two stories after a public outcry, but is still felt to, in the words of one guidebook, "dishonor" the quarter and the sky.

Meantime, the suburbs outside the ring road bristle with fanciful tall buildings, like the giant Grande Arche de La Défense, thirty-six stories high, built in the shape of an arch, on the axis of the Arc de Triomphe. To cross the Périphérique is to enter a brave new world of (usually ugly) mirrored skyscrapers and round or trapezoidal architectural fantasies.

THE MATERIAL WORLD

Inanimate objects, have you a soul
That's attached to our soul, with the strength to love?
Lamartine, HARMONIES

In Rue Bonaparte and the adjoining streets are a con-
centration of art and antiques galleries and stores mostly so grand I have been afraid to go into them, but once
or twice a year, the dealers have a sort of fair, and put
their most alluring objects in their windows. The
assortment boggles the mind—giant porphyry urns,
bits of antique tombs, Boulle cabinets, chandeliers,
antlers, paintings from various epochs.

Madame Boccador, one of the antiques dealers along
the Quai Voltaire to the west of Bonaparte, has a beautiful tapestry of Diane de Poitiers, or rather, Poitiers as
the goddess Diana, with Acteon, who has just been
turned into a stag for having looked upon the naked
beauty in her bath. His dog sits ominously at his side—
we know from the myth that his dog will soon kill him.

Madame Boccador, like everyone in St.-Germain, it seems, writes books. One day she gave me a volume of her stories; but her other works are about art. I learned two things from Madame Boccador, just as I always learn something when I walk around the neighborhood, whether I mean to or not: It had always escaped me that some of the statues of robed religious figures holding babies, ubiquitous in France and Italy, are not the Madonna but Christ himself. Their long hair and drapery had confused me; these are "Majesties," adult Christs holding baby Jesuses.

The other thing I learned is that though I had always thought that early painters just didn't know how to do children, in fact those wizened baby Jesuses that the Majesty or Madonna is holding in old paintings is to illustrate the idea that Christ was older and wiser than either his mother or mankind, and brought wisdom to us.

Madame Boccador specializes in art of the Middle Ages and Renaissance, venturing on this métier almost by accident, after starting medical studies—which she thinks ought to be a requirement for anyone interested in sculpture. Medical studies are an integral part of St.-Germain, with branches of the medical schools, the ancient hospitals, and the present Académie de Médicine all here, the latter on Rue Bonaparte, just on the other side of the École des

Galleries along Quai Malaquais

Beaux-Arts, handy for my husband, John, who is a corresponding member, to use its library.

Madame Boccador is one of many dealers in paintings and antique furniture on Rue Bonaparte and along the quays, art dealing a speciality of the neighborhood. I remember being struck, when I first came to France, by the abundance of decorative objects, their gold and crystal, their ormolu, and—to Americans, influenced by an aesthetic of Shaker simplicity—their overdone fanciness. The French eye, if one may generalize, has evolved a tolerance for the more complicated, even baroque, the gilded, that took me awhile to appreciate. It is the difference, say, between portraits of George Washington by Gilbert Stuart, and the famous portrait of Louis XIV in high heels with flowing curly wig. Never mind that Charles II wore similar wigs in England, those high heels are so French!

Is it possible to think of shopping as a cultural experience? I hope it is. It's fashionable to deplore the loss of bookstores in St.-Germain-des-Prés, and the arrival of the banal global brand-name boutiques. But it is still true that to look into the shops and galleries of this quarter is to pass in review the art of several centuries, the evolution of French decorative taste, mini-museums of African or folk or modern or medieval art—there is a gallery of contemporary Japanese art now, and, by the bus stop on Rue Bonaparte, of Indian and African old-ish kitsch that from time to time has in the window something irresistible. Once I bought a large African spoon, on a pedestal, like sculpture; and another time a crystal from India to dangle protectively around my neck. For a long time I've been in love with one dealer's North Indian—or Chinese?—porcelain parrots, but am deterred by their price and the fact that I want more than one, want a whole flock of them. Just as going to the flea market at the Porte de Clignancourt in Paris is to risk being overcome by the acres of Things—porcelain, wood carving, old picture frames, clothes, mirrors, statues, jewelry, boiseries, an infinitude of canvas and moldings, fireplaces, prints, sofas, tables, boars' heads, bedsteads, tusks, theatrical scenery, pieces out of ancient pubs ... so, too, is it overwhelming to go window shopping in this neighborhood.

The French have a different attitude to Things, and the accretion of centuries of Things is impressive, a recapitulation of history itself, compressed into a few showrooms, an abundance of the greatest examples of everything from every epoch (at overwhelming expense), a carnival of astounding connoisseurship. To begin with the Greek and Roman: There's little left of Greco-Roman Paris. There are the bits of the baths now incorporated into the Cluny Museum at Boulevard

St.-Germain and Boulevard St.-Michel (where you can also see "The Lady and the Unicorn," the charming series of tapestries), and an amphitheater, the much-restored Arènes de Lutece. But there is a lot more of Greco-Roman art for sale: There is a dealer on Rue Bonaparte, and another on the Rue des Sts.-Pères, who sell ancient busts and fragments, some so beautiful one is sure that the Greek or Italian governments ought to come after them. (Though, thinking of a visit we paid to our Greek friend Charis at his Santorini island summer place, where his yard was strewn with statues, dug up in the course of putting in a seawall, it appears that in Greece they have more than they know what to do with. If you dig up a statue in your garden in Greece, you notify the antiquities ministry, and they register it but tell you to keep it until they need it, which might be never.)

There must be a connection between the very noticeable French interest in material objects, witness their abundance of statuary, figurines, busts—three-dimensional objects rather than pictures—and their concern to dismantle things carefully, stone by stone. Someone bought the stones of the destroyed Bastille to build his château in the Midi. It is as if the French now have a more active sense than others of the material world as the potent manifestation of political and religious or other intangible conditions of life, perhaps because of their destructive mistakes during the Revolution?

Take the little carvings by Jean Goujon on the Anet doors of the chapel. We are all travelers, at heart if not in fact, and it is no secret that because we all travel at top speed, we are too apt to miss these tiny details, the odd felicities that derive from the accretions of centuries of civilization—or of savagery, of which this neighborhood has seen more than its share. In the Cour de Commerce, ten minutes' walk from Rue Bonaparte at Odéon, you can see the emplacement of the first guillotine, set up by Dr. Guillotin to practice on sheep, now marked by two little holes in the pavement.

For the visitor to Paris to think in terms of just one neighborhood is to miss the Arc de Triomphe, and the cemetery at Père-Lachaise, or Lafayette's grave in the Cimetière de Picpus; but there are almost certainly mysteriously quiet and charming things two steps from wherever the traveler happens to be staying that may better repay his attention than battling tourist crowds at the great monuments. A day spent climbing the Tour Eiffel and you will probably miss the four della Robbia medallions on the facade of the little building in the courtyard of one of the houses on the Quai Malaquais, around the corner from me, four portraits, garlanded and smiling—were they embedded in the plaster when the building was put up in 1630? Did they come there with the Italianate influence of the Médicis? Or are they the whim of some recent traveler? No one in the building is quite sure.

One day I went around the quartier looking only at doors and entrances, many listed on the register of protected sites in France, and all always indicative of the status of the former occupants, often carved, often crowned by statuary. Just to walk up and down any of the streets of St.-Germain looking only at these elements is to see things you have never seen before; the visual details of Parisian architecture in any quartier is so rich that sometimes this way of disciplined looking is the only way to begin to take it in.

Another focus might be only to look into courtyards. This is harder where there are door codes, but often these are off during the day; the only way to know is to walk along a Parisian street, punching the central buttons and entering the doors that give the reassuring little click. If someone questions what you are doing in his courtyard, say, *"Je fais une étude d'architecture."*

Talking of architecture: As everybody knows, Paris is bisected by the Seine River, broad, brisk, brown, and tamed between sumptuously tended banks and stone ramparts, walkways, arched over by forty bridges along the length of the city. During the First World War, the

American writer Edith Wharton, who lived not far from St.-Germain all through it, on the Rue Varenne in the Faubourg St.-Germain, and was a war heroine into the bargain, wrote a little booklet, *French Ways and Their Meaning,* to explain to people in America why French civilization was worth their fighting for. One of her reasons was the lovely way the French took care of their riverbanks, with pedestrian walkways, statues, cobblestone paths, and planting. She deplored our American habit of putting factories along the river and letting them dump their waste into them. She had other views as well, many of them quite critical of her native land, which, like Henry James, she left for good and never went back to.

The width of the Seine presented a challenge in medieval times, and even in the seventeenth century you mostly had to cross by ferry, though some bridges existed and would be swept away from time to time. D'Artagnan would have been able to cross on the Pont Neuf, the oldest bridge in Paris, looking today more or less as it did in the sixteenth century when it was begun (1578, finished in 1607). Henri IV and Marie de Médicis were there to inaugurate it, while Queen Margot would then have been overseeing the building of her house nearby. Many things have happened on the Pont Neuf since, including Pierre Curie being killed by a carriage, as he walked along, distracted, it is said, by Madame Curie's infidelity.

No one remembers this now, but I have seen swastikas hung on the Pont Neuf during a fifty-year commemoration of De Gaulle's speech to his countrymen from England in June of 1942. Now it was fifty years later, and the decor of the bridges was meant to re-create the city as it was during the Occupation, when the Parisians heard on their radios the words that they should and would resist. A copy of a radio set was put on top of the obelisk in the Place de la Concorde (where once there stood a guillotine!) and the speech broadcast again. Even fifty years later, it was chilling to see the Nazi banners, thrilling to hear the brave words.

The great event for the Pont Neuf in recent years was when the artist Christo wrapped it. Always beautiful, it was now swathed in a million yards of gold-colored canvas. Two little ladies on my bus said, "This government! What will they think of next? I suppose we the taxpayers are paying for this."

There are forty bridges in all, whereas as late as Napoleon's time there were only thirteen. Several of the nicest and most interesting bridges are those I see every day, the Pont Neuf, the Pont des Arts, the Pont du Carousel, and the Pont Royal. D'Artagnan wouldn't have seen the Pont des Arts, our nearest bridge, a footbridge leading from the Institut de France, just downriver from the Pont Neuf, over to the eastern wing of the Louvre. Wide and welcoming, it's the scene of art shows, strolling minstrels, joggers, tourists, and locals admiring the view up and down the river, people painting, pouring cocktails, or just hanging out. When Christo wrapped the Pont Neuf, we found the best view of it was from this bridge, where people hung over the railings exclaiming and snapping photos. The Pont des Arts was the first steel bridge, built by Napoleon Bonaparte in 1803.

More recently, the Pont des Arts itself was the scene of an amazing show of sculpture, larger-than-life figures made in mud, straw, and daub by an African sculptor, Ousmane Sow from Senegal. It was almost too creepy to walk across the bridge by moonlight, especially for an American, since the images evoked were of the American slaves, now seeming to come to life in positions of anguish, against the dark Parisian river.

Everywhere you look in Paris there are statues. They are an important part of the French decorative style. St.-Germain and all the bridges, and all of Paris, are peopled with huge figures in marble or bronze, even wood; busts in terra-cotta, bronze, plaster, marble, sometimes embellished with gold, giants several times life-size, tiny figurines ... for instance, the immense, inspiring statue of Henri IV on the Pont Neuf. A recent Houdon

exhibition at Versailles also brought some figures familiar to Americans—Lafayette, Franklin, Washington, who
all sat for the great sculptor. A Versailles curator told me
there are thousands of statues in the park and in the
reserves of that château alone.

Philip Trager's lovely book of photographs, *Changing
Paris,* captures these amazing presences on public buildings and bridges—Justice, Neptune, Lyons, the Seine,
Paris, Industry, Abundance—a population of exemplary
or mythological beings numerous enough to form a
city by themselves. The facades of the Louvre alone are
encrusted with hundreds of statues. At my nearest corner,
Quai Malaquais and Bonaparte, three: La République,
Voltaire, and Montesquieu. At the other end, outside Les
Deux Magots, a large cubist figure by Zadkine, and
Picasso's bust of Dora Maar in the little park across from
it. Often you pass without noticing them, wonderful statues posing as modest architectural elements holding up
porches or balconies or looming over lintels. There is a
beautiful building at 6 Rue des Sts.-Pères whose iron balcony is held up by four superb lions, who, blackened by
traffic fumes, are scarcely noticeable except when you specially look for them.

A Nod to the Belle Époque

In the old days, there were in Paris witnesses
to the majority of events I present here, and who
could have confirmed them, if you don't believe me.

Alexandre Dumas fils,

CAMILLE: LA DAME AUX CAMILIAS

In 1801, Bernard Germain-Étienne De La Ville, Comte de Lacépède, the biologist, who had left during the Revolution, was back in Paris, living in the apartment we live in now. Along with his scientific activities he was a senator, wrote two operas, and was widely admired. I wish his ghost were more palpable here in our rooms, since he was said to be a genius; but I don't really feel its presence, nor see his face in the mirrors in my living room that must have reflected him, too. Like Lacépède, many people had prospered after the Revolution. The landless bourgeoisie could buy property, or win it by lottery. It was the dawn of the nineteenth century.

In 1810, part of Rue Bonaparte, then still known as Rue des Petits-Augustins, received its present name; the whole street would not be called Bonaparte until 1852. Napoleon Bonaparte was the force, the event, the fascination of this period. As I live on the first floor, I gaze across at the windows of what by one tradition were the apartments of his sister Pauline, though Hillairet doesn't mention her. But it is certain that his first wife, Josephine, lived at 1-3 Rue des Petits-Augustins with her first husband, Beauharnais.

In the nineteenth century, Paris as a whole would achieve the look it generally has today, but only a few things happened to change St.-Germain-des-Prés, most notably the construction of the Boulevard St.-Germain and the "Haussmannian" apartment buildings that line it. But Haussmann was by no means responsible for all the changes; many had been made before. For instance, it was Napoleon I who in 1800 pulled down the Chapelle de la Vièrge of the Abbey to make the Rue de l'Abbaye.

An association with art and literature continued in this quartier. The Comédie-Française had had its birth on Rue Mazarine, one street over from Rue de Seine, where the works of Racine and Molière were first performed in the seventeenth century. Actresses lived in this area, most famously Voltaire's friend, poor Adrienne Lecouvreur, who died but was refused burial in a consecrated cemetery (on account of her godless ways) and so was cremated by her friends on a makeshift bier on the street. Legend has it that it was Voltaire himself who closed her eyes. Marechal de Saxe, the great-grandfather of George Sand, was another of her lovers.

By 1831, George Sand was living on the Rue de Seine, at number thirty-one, dressed like a man, trying to exist by painting tobacco cans and portraits in watercolor, and doing translations; the street she saw must have looked pretty much as it does today. Balzac worked on Rue Visconti. La Rochefoucauld's house, called Hôtel de la Rochefoucauld since he became famous in his time, was sold after the Revolution, and became a public bath. Rooms were rented in it, a Madame Ancelot held a literary salon there; then it was torn down, in 1825, and the Rue des Beaux-Arts constructed.

It is on that street that poor Oscar Wilde died in 1900, hounded out of England by legal problems to do with his homosexual misadventure with Lord Alfred Douglas, the son of the Marquis of Queensbury, in what was then a seedy, and now is a sumptuous, little hotel, L'Hôtel, decorated by Jacques Garcia. The present proprietors will show you the very room where Wilde died, or you can stay in it, and luxurious it is, with paneling and faux-malachite panels. If it is true that Wilde remarked of the wallpaper, on his deathbed, "One of us has to go," and if it had been in its present state—it is so pretty—he would not have had that excuse to die. Another remark ascribed to him, "I am dying beyond my means," would certainly be true today, with his room costing more than four hundred euros a night.

On the southern part of Rue Bonaparte, near the Jardin du Luxembourg, there had been a building at number eighty for Jesuit novices. These were evicted at the time of the Revolution and the place rented to the Masons, called by the French "le Grand-Orient." A sort of clandestine, maybe illegal thing then, Masonry is still, for the French, maybe for all Europeans, slightly different from American Masons, whom I have always thought of as stout, civic-minded gentlemen, like Elks and Moose, who enjoy a men's night out. For Europeans, it seems, Masons are a powerful quasi-subversive group of godless conspirators.

As the Baron Haussmann, the henchman at mid-century of Napoleon III, went about his work of tearing down quaint old things, changes had occurred next door to us at 14 Rue Bonaparte, the École des Beaux-Arts. And I shouldn't fail to mention that by standing on the Quai Malaquais in 1871, we would have seen the flames in the sky of the burning of the Tuileries and the Hôtel de Ville just across the river in the uprising of the Commune; but St.-Germain did not burn.

This was the period of the great courtesans, immortalized in Dumas's (fils) play *La Dame aux Camilias,* or in Verdi's opera *La Traviata,* or even in later works like Collette's *Gigi.* However, unlike the actresses of the eighteenth century, in the 1800s these ladies lived in the eighth and sixteenth and other arrondissements to the west. The tradition of kept women was well alive into the twentieth century (and, for all I know, is still alive); the figure of Liane de Pougy (1869–1950) comes to mind, who had a great career in the Belle Époque, but lived on to become a lover of American Natalie Clifford Barney, around the corner at 20 Rue Jacob; and, eventually, a nun.

Nos Jours

I think perhaps I have gotten more out of life than it contains.
Natalie Clifford Barney

The twentieth century. Existentialism! Replaced by structuralism, deconstruction, Marxist criticism, Lacanianism, communism: Something of the local spirit of debate still seems to be alive that flourished with the scholastics and abbots of centuries ago, and the sixth arrondissement still claims to be its home, damped down during the two wars, to be sure. France suffered horribly in the first war, when it lost a sizable proportion of its young men. Many Americans stayed in Paris throughout that war—Edith Wharton, for example. Wharton, the American novelist, had spent most of her adult life in Europe. Now she worked herself to exhaustion and spent much of her own fortune organizing hostels for refugees, shelters for Belgian orphans of war, sewing enterprises to provide clothes to and earn money for the war effort, and after the war got the Légion d'Honneur, the prestigious decoration, for her service.

After the war, people reacted with the gaiety reflected in the expatriates living on the French Riviera in the twenties (as in Fitzgerald's *Tender is the Night*). Paris offered two things it had always offered, sexual freedom and drink, both in short supply at home. Americans who had always come to France for culture and clothes, now came for the wine, too, and apparently they have always come as sexual tourists. But the effects of Prohibition shouldn't be overlooked, especially among American men of letters who were or would become alcoholics— Hemingway, Faulkner, Fitzgerald, to name a few who came to France and lived in St.-Germain-des-Prés.

To talk of the sexual freedom of those days, something of history may explain the climate for women in St.-Germain in the 1920s, when expatrate lesbians had a sort of colony or social circle centered on Rue Jacob. It goes back, as I've suggested, to Queen Margot, and no doubt before: By the time the historical Marguerite (like Dumas's fictional one) was married to Henri of Navarre, she had been the mistress of a leading Catholic courtier, Henri de Guise, and before that of the Vicomte de Martigues, for several years, without particular detriment to her future. This seems to imply considerably greater sexual freedom for women, at least royal women, in the sixteenth century than would be the case later, though the rules were already changing, and had a setback under the sway of the Huguenots, when Parisian brothels were briefly closed.

Sexual freedom was allied to power, of course. Margot's mother effectively ruled France, as people said that Diane de Poitiers had done earlier. Queen Margot, her mother, and other royal women of her time, had, relative to later generations, a lot of power and status, as long as they didn't impinge too much on masculine prerogatives. My impression is that this could still describe the position of women in France: high, higher than in Anglo-Saxon countries—but not high enough seriously to challenge masculine prerogatives. And it also seems that French women of the seventeenth century had more freedom and more power than they would later. Catherine de Médicis, however, thought the days of her own youth were even better.

Queen Margot tells one story about a discussion with her mother on the subject of women's freedom. It has come up because evil intriguers, trying to stir up trouble between Margot and her husband, arrange for it to appear that she is improperly visiting a man; her carriage is parked outside his house, to be seen by her husband Henri as he and King Henri III drive by. "My carriage was easily to be distinguished, as it was gilt and lined with yellow velvet trimmed with silver."

Her husband Henri (because her husband was King of Navarre when they married, Queen Margot in her memoirs is obliged to refer to him as "the King my husband," to distinguish him from "the King my brother") is not upset, but Queen Margot's mother, Catherine de Médicis, gives her hell anyway when she hears about the outing, until she is reassured that there was nothing improper in Queen Margot's behavior; then she apologizes for her hasty condemnation of her daughter: "In my younger days," said she, "we were allowed to converse freely with all the gentlemen who belonged to the King our father, the Dauphin, and Monsieur d'Orleans, your uncles." It was normal for them to assemble in the bedchambers of court women, and nothing was thought of it. "Neither ought it to appear strange that Bussi sees my daughter in the presence of her husband's servants.... You are unfortunate to live in these times." Then she and her friends reminisce about "the pleasures and innocent freedoms of the times they had seen, when scandal and malevolence were unknown at Court."

What's sauce for the goose is sauce for the gander. The man, Bussy d'Amboise, later was rumored as Queen Margot's lover, and/or that of Madame de Sauves—and that of Margot's brother Henri, too. It's certain that the lot of a queen was not easy. Just as her mother Catherine had to put up with her husband's

Janet Flanner and Ernest Hemingway in Les Deux Magots during WWII

mistresses, including the fabled Diane de Poitiers, so did Queen Margot have to hold her tongue at Henri IV's constant affairs. But at least she had plenty of her own. Is it too much to believe that these powerful seventeenth-century Frenchwomen were the real ancestresses of notable women of our day, say, Simone de Beauvoir or Adrienne Monniers? Such geneologies are always a little facile, but the idea is defensible.

But to return to the elegant lesbians of the twenties, a friend of mine was taken by Janet Flanner to meet

Natalie Clifford Barney, who, having come to Paris in 1909, was still holding court in the early sixties on the Rue Jacob, at number twenty, where a little temple of "friendship" still stands in the garden, and where Mata Hari is said to have danced. Flanner hoped my friend would behave well—cautioning him that Barney was "the pope of lesbians," a remark made originally by Jean Cocteau. My friend reports that she was somewhat vague, but impressive, lying on a banquette of white bamboo in her garden near the temple of friendship.

Barney was beautiful and rich, and gathered around her a powerful, arty circle, people like Joyce, Flanner, of course, and Colette, and longtime friend the painter Romaine Brooks. The following list from a website devoted to her, of people who ate the cucumber (some say chicken) sandwiches and drank the champagne at her Friday salons, is worth quoting for its informative roster of Parisian figures:

Auguste Rodin, Rainer Maria Rilke, Colette, James Joyce, Paul Valéry, the Sitwell siblings, Pierre Loüys, Anatole France, Count Robert de Montesquiou, Edna St. Vincent Millay, Gertrude Stein, Alice B. Toklas, W. Somerset Maugham, T. S. Eliot, Ford Madox Ford, Isadora Duncan, Ezra Pound, Virgil Thomson, Jean Cocteau, Max Jacob, André Gide, William Carlos Williams, Djuna Barnes, George Antheil, Janet Flanner, Nancy Cunard,

Peggy Guggenheim, Mina Loy, Caresse and Harry Crosby, Marie Laurencin, Oscar Milosz, Paul Claudel, Adrienne Monnier, Sylvia Beach, F. Scott and Zelda Fitzgerald, Sinclair Lewis, Emma Calvé, Sherwood Anderson, Hart Crane, Alan Seeger, Mary McCarthy, Truman Capote, Françoise Sagan, and Marguerite Yourcenar.

Hemingway is missing here—did he never meet this remarkable woman, true descendant of Marguerite de Navarre? He was a great friend of Sylvia Beach, another of the famous lesbians of St.-Germain, with her renowned bookshop Shakespeare and Company, and her role in publishing James Joyce. Beach's partner Adrienne Monniers has in some ways always interested me more, maybe because she was such a good writer. The very first Shakespeare and Company was not on the Rue de l'Odéon but on the Rue Dupuytren, at number two—some American friends happen to live in that building now and have an old photo of the two women standing in their doorway under the sign. The more famous incarnation of Shakespeare and Company was at 12 Rue de l'Odéon, the street that runs from the Boulevard St.-Germain to the Théâtre de l'Odéon, the theater built in 1782 and still in operation, along with its small salle, Petit Odéon, for short plays by Becket or Brecht, sometimes in English.

That wonderful writer and bookshop owner Adrienne Monnier stayed in Paris during the second war, like her friend Sylvia Beach. Monnier tells the story of when, after the war, Hemingway comes to see them, he offers to save her from reprisals if she has collaborated at all—and she, examining her conscience, finds that she has not collaborated at all. No one is sure about Gertrude Stein, however, who did leave Paris for a village outside, but, though Jewish, survived the war nicely.

Barney, Beach, Flanner, Stein—these women left America for an unconventional and unconstricted life in Paris. So did countless other Americans, just as they had been doing since the eighteenth century, though in the twenties, they also came for alcohol. I've already recommended Brian N. Morton's amusing book *Americans in Paris,* which gives the impression that nothing has changed since the founding of America; there has been at any given moment a large circle or set of Americans who may or may not know each other back in the States but who socialize here, as true for the very French-oriented Edith Wharton as for people today. It was Adams and Franklin, or it was Edna St. Vincent Millay and Natalie Clifford Barney. Not that all the Americans in Paris like each other; Edith Wharton, for instance, disapproved of fellow expatriate Elsie de Wolfe, the American decorator, she who famously remarked of the Parthenon, "It's my color, beige!" But was it de Wolfe's lesbianism or her racy language that incurred Wharton's disapproval?

Paris affects the American visitors, but it does not seem that they affect Paris very much. It keeps on being French, which is the point of coming here. As for going back to the U.S., it almost seems that it was unwise to do so. Many people had trouble fitting back in—Hemingway and Fitzgerald, to name two. The wisest, once finding themselves here, stayed here—like Stein and Toklas, Barney, Flanner, and countless others, who slip into an American overlay of the French scene, transparent presences in an almost independent parallel world, discussing American politics and movies, American books, throwing up their hands at the intricacies of French politics, disputing or not the (recent) French disapproval of American politics, which they also don't really understand: "Explain your Electoral College again, *s'il vous plaît.*" "Why would you impeach someone for that?"

Beside Sylvia Beach, some others were here during the Second World War, when Paris was occupied by the Germans—for instance, poor Morton Fullerton, Edith Wharton's lover, living on in his unheated garret; poor

Matilda Gay, widowed, her château outside Paris occupied by Germans; she died, old and ill, to the sound of the Nazi boots tromping through her rooms. (She was an aunt of my friend Charlotte, herself another instance of someone with a French first name, who lives here with her French husband.) Matilda Gay was married to the American painter Walter Gay, who earned a good living with his charming portraits of people's rooms and furniture.

Though the Germans didn't seem to take too much of an interest in St.-Germain-des-Prés, many were billeted in the Lutetia Hotel, on the border of the sixth arrondissement in the seventh, and there are too many of those sad and moving plaques showing spots where someone *"mort pour la France"* and people still put flowers. The Germans did have a look in at Gertrude Stein's apartment on the Rue de Fleurus, and apparently scoffed at her Picassos.

More than three hundred years before, Queen Margot had observed that "captivity and its consequent solitude afforded me the double advantage of exciting a passion for study, and an inclination for devotion, advantages I had never experienced during the vanities and splendour of my prosperity." The Occupation seems to have had something of that effect on Picasso, Sartre, Beauvoir, and other artists and writers, who worked well during the war. Unmolested, Sartre and Simone de Beauvoir began coming to the Flore when their usual hangout in Montmartre was closed. Unlike most private apartments during the shortage of fuel, the Flore was warm, famously heated by a big stove. Beauvoir recounted her stratagems for getting a seat near it—one being to get up early and be there by opening time. Sartre lived for a time above the Café Bonaparte, where a friend of mine from Texas has rented an apartment now.

We were in Paris on the day Sartre died, in 1980, and were planning to have dinner with Mary McCarthy and her husband, who were delayed by French television, which wanted a comment from her. She said she was speechless, though, because they kept prompting "wasn't he a giant? Isn't it the loss of a giant?" and she kept thinking about how short he was; her fabled propensity for blurting out the truth left her with nothing to say.

The renowned "golden age" of St.-Germain-des-Prés came after the Second World War. It was then that Marie-Claude went to the Nuages, Dany Simon went to the Tabou, and saw, or knew, all the legendary characters. They went to lectures by Roland Barthes or Georges Bataille, bought jewelry from a glamorous Swedish baronness called Torun, ate when they could afford it at the Petit St.-Benoît. Marguerite Duras lived on the Rue St.-Benoît at that period, and went to Communist meetings at the Bonaparte—both of these places still in existence. Sometimes, having coffee at the Bonaparte (at the corner of Bonaparte and Rue Guillaume-Apollinaire), I can almost hear, in the animated French conversations going on around me, Duras and her comrades arguing the urgent party issues that consumed them.

The seriousness with which French intellectuals and artists took communism is perhaps hard for Americans to grasp, so entrenched were we in our official national fear of it. (Whatever one's individual experience: I was someone, no doubt typical of many Midwesterners, who had never met either a communist, or until recently even a Russian, and to whom, therefore, communism was too remote and abstract to seem a credible danger.) Marguerite Duras has described the bitter quarrels over such things as sincerity that kept earnest young party faithful bickering late over coffee or brandy at the Bonaparte about who was in or who was out of their cadre.

Another successful hangout in the fifties was the Bar Vert on the Rue Jacob, where you went between ten and midnight. My friend the painter says that it eventually became a tourist attraction—people stood outside to glimpse the beautiful people who appeared on schedule as they made their nightly rounds. They were ogled because an enterprising journalist published their itinerary, which caused them to abandon it and move on to other places.

Another of these was the Royal St.-Germain, in the spot where Emporio Armani is now, at the corner of Rue de Rennes and Boulevard St.-Germain; in the intervening phase the famous Drugstore was there, a place to buy anything, open around the clock. There is still a jazz club near here on Rue St.-Benoît. My husband John and Robert Gottlieb, the famous editor, went there one night and reported that it was serious, staid—a serious jazz-listening experience, no dancing. But the Tabou is long gone—or not so long, for though the spirit died by the early fifties, the place dragged on as a tourist sight til the early nineties. Former denizens of the Tabou were scornful at a re-creation of it the other night for French television. It showed a capacious suite of underground cellars, caves, but "the real Tabou was miniscule," they said.

I haven't figured out exactly where it can have been, unless it was at the site of what is now Ruby, or Vodka, two clubs near that address. Inside Ruby, everyone was African, and *champagne maison* started at 169 euros the bottle. From their astonishment that we, a mild American couple, might want to come in, we inferred there was a second agenda, but I don't know what; it was not a simple bar.

The Tabou was at 33 Rue Dauphine, down in the caves for the chic, and upstairs, Boris Vian, popular playwright and novelist says, in his *Manual of St.-Germain-des-Prés,* for "Swedes, American communists with guitars and GI spectacles, English queers etc."—i.e. the squares. Communism, however, went on being chic, in fact the only possible political philosophy for the fashionable young. There was a dress code, according to Vian: for men, brush cuts, long and curly in front, shirts open to the navel, colorful socks, and for women long hair, no lipstick. The fashionable existentialists looked, to modern eyes, like the cast of *Happy Days* or figures from a James Dean movie.

There are still plenty of bars, in the American or English sense, as well as cafés where you can get a *coup de rouge* or a brandy with your coffee in the morning, but you never see the public drunkenness so common in England in and outside their pubs. The cafés of this neighborhood—Café de Flore and Les Deux Magots being the most famous—are always filled, all the time, with people drinking tea, coffee or cocoa, or a glass of wine, and having a bite to eat at mealtime. I usually go to the Tabac des Beaux-Arts on the quay, less crowded, and happily located at the foot of Rue Bonaparte, thus, the closest to home, and with a view out on the little place with the statue of the Republic overlooking the river.

Apparently there weren't a lot of drugs in old St.-Germain; what there was was opium, for the elderly addicts of Colette's generation still around. The main narcotic was the sense of freedom that followed the war. Then, as today, you went to the Flore or Les Deux Magots as a fierce partisan of one but not the other. Boris Vian, tells the story of two couples, constrained by circumstances from going to their habitual Flore, who ran into each other at Les Deux Magots and became wildly excited—"What are you doing here!"—as if they had met by chance in some foreign land.

REAL LIFE

Bouquinistes *line this side of the Seine, between the Pont du*
Carousel and the Pont de la Tournelle. After a stop on the
Pont des Arts to browse through the stalls on the quai de
Conti under the watchful eye of Condorcet, go down to the
quayside, away from the noise and bustle of the street to con-
template the timeless views of the square du Vert-Galant, the
Pont-Neuf and the towers of Notre Dame.

from the MICHELIN GUIDE TO PARIS

J. and I have settled into the cheerful life of the neighborhood. One of the things about St.-Germain is still
that, because of its village quality, you run into people,
or see people, you recognize. Catherine Deneuve is the
most likely sighting of the truly famous around here
these days. I've seen her twice in restaurants, a beautiful
woman, slightly thickening in the middle, which is of
course endearing, since she must be sixty. Lauren Bacall
is often seen in the Flore, and once I saw her in the
Monoprix, buying a present; I heard this strangely

familiar voice, speaking French but with a strong American accent, looked over, and it was she.

Every day I must go get groceries from the Rue de Buci, the Monoprix, or the Grande Épicerie. Buy a new Métro pass at the beginning of each month. Take walks, to note the changes of season, something California lacks. On Thursday nights the art galleries have openings along the Rues de Seine and Bonaparte. Americans have potluck suppers and events organized around the political situation back home or cooperative efforts for other ends. My California friend Ellery helps me set up my wi-fi network, but I'm not sure how I can be useful to him in turn. Our American world is, as it always has been, a world within a world, more or less invisible to the real inhabitants.

From my kitchen window I notice that La Voisine's hair is "going back." Once a cheerful reddish brown, it is turning gray at the roots; whether she is letting it grow out or has just put off going to the hairdresser remains to be seen. When we meet on the street she does not acknowledge our back fence relationship or even seem to recognize me. Is this French good manners or something else?

Looking out my windows in one direction I see the chapel, but out the front window, I look onto the smart shops of Rue Bonaparte. Besides the *antiquaires* and art dealers and book dealers around here, there are specialists in interior decoration. Far from being white paint and gilt, the French "look" of the moment seems to derive from Milan and to feature things like lampshades and lamp bases that are now rectangular where they used to be round. The wood is black, the upholstery gray, beige, or leather. Exceptions to this are to be found on the Rue Jacob and the Place de Furstemberg, where there are several maisons that deal in good reproductions of traditional shapes of furniture, silver plate, lamps, and so on. One of these, Flamant, is in fact Belgian, recalling that the French are fond of saying, with a sigh, that the best French food is now found in Belgium. There are fabric stores—French like Pierre Frey, Italian Rubelli, English Colefax and Fowler, and so on. Of interest to an American is that, unlike at home, where you have to have a decorator buy these things for you, here you can just go in and order them yourself.

One of the most famous decorators in the neighborhood was Madeleine Castaing, who had a shop at the corner of Bonaparte and Jacob, now mostly taken over by the elegant *pâtisserie* and *salon du thé* Ladurée. When Ladurée, expanding from their original branch had bought the space and were remodeling, they tore away Madelaine Castaing's sign, only to find underneath a beautiful earlier sign in glass and gold reading "pâtisserie," which they retained and restored, taking it as an omen that they were meant to be there.

Madame Castaing was known for her eccentricities—her black wig was held on by a face-lifting chin strap so that she looked like an ancient drum majorette—and also for bringing to the attention of the French bourgeoisie the nineteenth-century decorative style now called by the name of Napoleon III, the mid-nineteenth-century emperor. (His rooms in the Louvre are open to be seen, opulent in red plush and mahogany, gilded boiseries, crystal chandeliers.) We might perhaps call Madame Castaing's taste Victorian, and indeed she brought Staffordshire dogs and English furniture over for her clients, causing a little vogue for *le style anglais*. When she retired to her country place, the filmmakers James Ivory and Ismail Merchant bought her apartment and with it some of the furniture, not without noting, though, her extortionist prices, which you can still pay, at her shop on Rue Jacob.

This returns me to the tremendous world of French decorative objects. Madame Laloup, on the Quai Malaquais (or *mal acquis,* according to etymologists), has furnished a number of sumptuous African pieces for the Louvre and the former Museum of Oceanic

Arts, but is planning on giving up her life as a dealer. "I dunno," she says, "I've had it with art—I have six pieces in the African section of the Louvre over there. But, it's getting too difficult to find things, and I'm too tired to haggle. I'm closing down. I think I'll open a pâtisserie, something like that, in this space. I own the space...."

Her space, by the way, is in the seventeenth-century Hôtel de Transylvanie, the grand brick-and-stone building on the corner of Bonaparte and the Quai Malaquais, dating from 1622, and named after a Transylvanian prince who rented it in the eighteenth century.

Talking of pâtisseries and Ladurée reminds of the war of the macaroons, a lively discussion held among Parisians partial to either those made by Ladurée, by the other long-established pâtissiers Dalloyau, or Gérard Mulot on the Rue de Seine, or by the chic Pierre Hermé, former pastry chef at Ladurée who left to open his own smart shop on Rue Bonaparte, or by some particular favorite of other neighborhoods. I've never been into the Pierre Hermé shop because there is always a line out the door. (Though I saw him once, eating with some other chefs at Hélène Darroze, an elegant restaurant on Rue d'Assas, and, if I may say so, his enormous girth threw a scare into me about ever eating one of his concoctions.)

French macaroons, by the way, are not those coconut-almond cookies we think of, but a sort of pastel-colored oreo, two halves of pastry with a filling in between, in various flavors and sizes—pistachio, caramel, chocolate, *fraises* ... or even chili, or oyster. The more fanciful the flavors the better.

I have to admit I stand in line like the rest at Ladurée, but not for macaroons; I like the lemon tarts and *religieuses,* and for special Sunday mornings, the croissants. There is a woman I often see there who sometimes buys nine huge boxes of pastries on Sunday mornings, as if she were godmother to an orphanage.

When American friends ask me how I can bear to live in France, with its lack of supermarkets and parking lots, I can only gloat about the pleasures of the Grande Épicerie, a sort of supermarket, perhaps the world's fanciest, apart from Harrod's Food Hall in London, or the amazing German KaDeWe in Berlin. The Grande Épicerie is fifteen minutes' walk into the seventh arrondissement to the Bon Marché, and the Bon Marché is the main Left Bank department store. Such stores were a French invention of the nineteenth century; for a sense of their history, evolving from the small boutiques that still form the basis of French commerce, you should read Émile Zola's novel *Au Bonheur des Dames.* A few years ago, the Bon Marché was a slightly funky catch-all general store—you could buy paint and hardware, sewing supplies, shoes, dog food.

Now it has reinvented itself into elegance, after the fashion of the times, and features upscale ready-to-wear and furniture. I regret the loss of the former convenient features, but it's a treat to cruise the glamorous stuff they have now. Of course, it's approximately the same as is found in San Francisco, which also has a Cristofle, a Cartier, and all the other main French brands, just as Paris has Gap and Levi's. Everyone who travels complains of the same thing: the sameness of shopping no matter where.

Purses are sold in all countries, but there seem to be more here. And who was the observant person who wrote of French women that all their purses seem to be new? It's true that *Parisiennes* seem quite preoccupied with the handbag—witness their luxury brands, like Hermès, Louis Vuitton, or Longchamps. This emphasis seems to be an offshoot of the Parisian lifestyle that requires you to carry a lot of stuff around, so that a handbag becomes important beyond its looks and fashionableness.

At first I resisted implementing the Parisian practice of little trolleys, handbags on wheels, with which to transport the daily requirement of groceries. I have been told these are unthinkable in New York, but everyone in Paris uses them, and I immediately saw why. I have one that converts to a backpack for taking it with you to the store; it then reverts to a wheeled state for coming home with heavy bottles and cat sand.

I had lunch a week or two ago with the American art dealer Darthea Speyer, whose famous gallery is on the Rue Jacques-Callot, a little street at right angles to the Rue de Seine. This was the first gallery of surrealist art, in the twenties. Madame Speyer took it over in the fifties and has stayed here ever since. She comes from Pittsburgh. She must have known Raymond Duncan, Isadora's brother (who was brought up in Berkeley, lived on Rue Mazarine, and wore togas and sandals), and lots of the other Americans who stayed.

From time to time one is afforded this sort of glimpse backward in time. The other night we wandered into the little restaurant La Brochetterie on the Rue St.-Benoît, a tiny place on two floors, maybe ten tables in all, that seems to exist in a kind of fifties time warp. Near us a young man in a black turtleneck, with a guitar case under his table, smoking to be sure, we heard to say, *"Dieu existe, tu sais...."* God exists.

I sometimes wonder if the esprit, gaiety, intellectual seriousness, and serious stylishness of the earlier period was the reflex of poverty and shared hardship. Maybe these privations are a precondition to gaiety and joy, moods that seem unavailable to twentieth-century

Americans and French alike. La Brochetterie, by the way, is one of the few places in the neighborhood to get something halfway decent to eat. During the war, when food was scarce except for rutabagas and bits of meat, the Petit St.-Benoît, across from La Brochetterie, was somehow serving cheap meals, and is still there, still cheap, but not actually very good. I also find myself wondering if the food was any better in the old days?

French food is delicious, but there are neighborhoods better than this one to find it in. The French say the declining standard of the food is the fault of tourists, who evidently are less demanding than real French people, allowing them to get by with indifferent food. On the same street as La Brochetterie, Rue St.-Benoît, I used to like the Dedicace, which was relatively new, a large space and hence often rather forlornly empty, and now seemingly vanished.

I'm speaking of "French" restaurants. As happened in England, Italians have made a difference in the neighborhood food—I can think of four really good Italian restaurants—Marco Polo, Vicolo, Armani (the best of them, actually, in, yes, the Armani boutique, upstairs), and a cozy little one, Monteverdi. And there are a lot of others, it's just that we haven't tried them. When we're truly homesick, we go to the City Zen on the Rue de Seine for a really good hamburger, or Coffee Parisien, next to the important Village Voice Bookshop on Rue Princess. Coffee Parisien is owned by the son of my late friend Rita, who was run over by a bus, that archetypal fate. We all imagined she was in danger on her bicycle, a woman in her eighties, but this time she was on foot; how we wished she had been on her bike.

People get attached to their native food. The French and Americans alike all used to love the Restaurant des Beaux-Arts on Rue Bonaparte, charmingly old-timey, with its plump, tired waitresses. When it was replaced by a really trashy art gallery (bronze sheep), well-dressed French people walking by were stunned that such a thing could change, and shook their fists, shouting *"honteux, honteux"*—"shame, shame," at the embarrassed construction workers.

The anglophone in this quarter has two choices of where to go for books, the Village Voice Bookshop, run by Odile Hellier, a knowledgeable Frenchwoman who studied American literature at Berkeley, and the San Francisco Bookshop on the Rue de l'Odéon for secondhand books. There is also still the Shakespeare and Company, named after the famous bookshop run in the thirties by Sylvia Beach and Adrienne Monnier, but the new avatar is in the fifth arrondissement, and so dusty I got out of the habit of going there because of sneezing fits. I have been told that Sylvia Whitman (named for Sylvia Beach), the new young manager, has dusted. There is also a Canadian-run bookshop in the fifth arrondissement, Abbey Books, so no lack of books in English.

Walking over to the Village Voice takes me by a number of thrilling specialty bookshops on the Rue Bonaparte, including two in this very building or next door: the Porte Étroite, a tiny place which is actually underneath La Voisine's courtyard and sells art books; and the bookshop of M. Rossignol, a drawn, silent-looking person whom I meet in the foyer of our building as he checks his mail. In the window of Monsieur Rossignol's bookshop as I write, is an autographed letter by Henri IV, his hand authoritative, assured, genial, royal, only the slightly faded ink and odd *S*'s suggesting another era, but hardly more than four centuries. I inquired, but he had nothing from the hand of Queen Margot.

The drawback of all these bookstores for me is, of course, that the books are in French, but apart from that, it is bliss just looking in the windows at the wonderful things that could be read, if only I didn't read French so slowly. (Except for books by Georges Simenon; I buy Inspector Maigret mysteries from the bouquinistes on the quays.) Never mind, books lend the tone to the neighborhood that it long has had, of intellectuals and debates, forgotten knowledge, the elaborate appreciation of their culture that the French have and write about, sometimes so boringly, even when, as Edmund White points out in *The Flâneur,* "Paris itself has become a cultural backwater," and St.-Germain is like "a beatnik brat [who] has grown up to be an elegant and rather brainless matron."

Nonetheless, most of French publishing is clustered around here in the fifth or sixth arrondissements, and here is where the writers tend to live, only the ones that can afford it, alas. My last novel came out from a publisher called Ramsay, on the little street Rue St.-André des Arts, across from an ancient building associated in the fourteenth century with the Navarres, the family who would rule in the south, become Protestants, and produce Henri IV. My new French publisher, Buchet-Chastel, looks out on the Place de l'Odéon, also in the sixth.

I think I have described how if, when I leave my building, instead of turning right toward St.-Germain, I turn left out the front door, we are perhaps a hundred yards from the river, and at the corner one can either turn left toward the Quai Voltaire, where Voltaire lived, and the Musée d'Orsay, or else turn right along the Quai Malaquais toward the Institut de France and the Bibliothèque Mazarine. I might just finish this essay by suggesting a little walk in this direction.

Facing the quay in this short block, the first two buildings were built around 1630. Number seven now houses a *tabac* on the ground floor, the Tabac des Beaux-Arts, (which is more of a café than a tabac, as it also serves food), which has been there for more than a hundred and fifty years. The current proprietor and his wife are proud of this tradition, and have shared their papers about it with me, photocopied from the *Bulletin de la Société historique du VIème Arrondissement,* Tome XXXVIII, année 1938. (They are too young to remember André Breton, whom a friend of mine often used to see in their tabac in the fifties, having a drink with other intellectuals and artists; but they know a lot about the neighborhood of today.)

Reading the history of their building, just that building alone, you see that in the 375 years it has been there, it's been the scene of at least five hundred personal histories, each with its private anguishes, marital and fiscal disasters, joys, no doubt, and endless legal entanglements, enough for dozens of novels. Just a few of the names: Monsieur de Garsanlan; the Marquis de Mirabel; an English diplomat, Isaac Wake, who was renting but died of a fever; to be replaced by a

Tabac on Quai Malaquais

Dutchman, Hugues de Groot, imprisoned; Guillaume Brisacier, a con man and illegitimate son of Brisacier; Paul and André Verani de Varennes; Monsieur and Madame La Fosse; Marie de St.-Simon, who married René de Cordouan but had the marriage annulled for impotence; Monsieur Alagille, bourgeois ...

The next building, number five, belonged to the same seventeenth-century owner, Jacques de Garsanlan, who also built number seven. If you walk into the number seven courtyard, look into the foyer in the passage on the right, at the beautiful staircase. Up it climbed the former residents, including the ubiquitous Marechal de

Saxe, great-grandfather of George Sand, and Baroness Korff, a Swedish friend of Marie-Antoinette's presumed lover Count Ferson, who was renting it before the Revolution. The baroness and others, appalled by the mounting savagery of the dawning catastrophe, conspired to help get Louis XVI a passport so he could escape, though he didn't.

Number three, built around the same time as the others, has a little house in the courtyard, on which the four small della Robbia medallions have been mounted. Number one was part of Queen Margot's house, but this wing was torn down.

All three buildings in this row have housed numberless foreign diplomats, for St.-Germain has always drawn étrangers who had the luck to find themselves here. For the thousandth time, I reflect on why I myself am here, an unexpected fate. In coming with a husband who had work here, liking it, and settling in, I am in the same situation, probably, as the Baroness Korff. All of Paris is filled with foreigners whose story is the same, brought here by chance, staying on. For some people, living in exotic distant places is normal, but John and I never expected to. What luck that life does not turn out exactly as we expect.

So, finally, I cannot escape the idea that St.-Germain-des-Prés, French as it is, is also ourselves, the foreigners who have always been here. And, if you have always been here, can you be foreign? St.-Germain-des-Prés, in extending its welcome, seems to know that its strangers are part of the whole.

As to the question of what is eluding us at home—it is perhaps that which Americans go home to address. Little has been written about the answer. Maybe it is one of those questions that is unanswerable, and though I have my own views, those are not the subject of these notes.

Apologia

When I began to write about St.-Germain-des-Prés, I had the naive idea that it would be possible to characterize it in the suggested 200 pages or so. I soon realized that one could easily write 200 pages on each of the buildings on my street, or on just the statues of the neighborhood, or only on the magnificent and ancient abbey church itself. To recount the rich history of this quarter, describe the abundant details of its architecture, try to convey its beauty, suggest its meaning to others, mention the fascinating characters who have lived here—all this defies brevity; some principle of selection was called for. This, then, is a subjective account of the things that bear upon my own daily life in St.-Germain-des-Prés, with apologies that of necessity I fall short of presenting the whole with anything like a guidebook's comprehensiveness. Yet I hope an account of the history and traditions that have created this urban marvel will be helpful in looking at other bridges or buildings beyond those I am speaking of and all the places I haven't space to include.

There are numberless books about Paris. Among the many I have profited from consulting, the following have been especially useful, and may be so to the reader, chief among them Jacques Hillairet's *Dictionnaire Historique des Rues de Paris,* a compendious and heavy two volumes of history and architectural detail that exist also in a paperback abridgement, *Connaissance du Vieux Paris,* that makes an invaluable companion on any walk in any neighborhood of the city. The (green) *Guide Michelin* for Paris is helpful and well organized, and there are numerous books of Parisian walks to be enjoyed, all covering roughly the same historic places, each discovering one or two offbeat surprises that differ from others. And Brian N. Morton's *Americans in Paris* is a fascinating door-to-door look at the Paris of our American forebears. I have used the Gutenberg project edition of Queen Margot's memoirs in an 1813 translation, as well as her *Memoires et Lettres* (London, 1966). Other books are mentioned in the text, among them

Leonard Pitt's photos in *Promenades dans le Paris disparu,* Steven Barclay's anthology *A Place in the World Called Paris,* Boris Vian's *Manual of St.-Germain-des-Prés,* the various works of Zola and Dumas, Joseph Roth's *Report from a Parisian Paradise,* Edmund White's *Le Flâneur,* and many more. And above all, Emmanuel Schwartz's *La Chapelle de l'École des Beaux-Arts de Paris,* the only book about the chapel, the origin of this essay.

Acknowledgments

I hardly know how to begin thanking the many people who have helped with this book; lots of friends have pitched in with ideas and anecdotes and have lent me books and photos. I'd like to mention in particular the French ones, for I'm sure it must have required extra patience on their part to fill in a backward American on all the things a French person already knows: Mme. Philippe Aghion, Annick Baudoin, Mr. M. N. Bodiansky, Marie-Claude de Brunhoff, M. and Mme. E. de Bresson, David and Marcel Fleiss, the Fourest family, Hélène Maury, the staff of the Bibliothèque Mazarine, that of the Tabac des Beaux-Arts, Maître Jean-Jacques Ploquin,

Mme. V. Debieuvre; and then, American friends who know a lot about the neighborhood: Mary Blume, Leonard Pitt, Arthur Hall Smith, Sally Williams-Allen, Drusilla Walsh. From afar, Diana Ketcham. Members of my family: two architects—Amanda Johnson and her husband, architect Jean-François Blassel—and art historian Darcy Tell have clarified various architectural mysteries for me. John Murray has been a cheerful companion on neighborhood walks. I've mentioned in the text and afterward a number of books that have been invaluable. It goes without saying that mistakes are mine alone.

DIANE JOHNSON is a bestselling novelist, travel writer, and essayist. She holds a Ph.D. from UCLA and is the author of the National Book Award–nominated *Lesser Lives* and *Le Divorce,* as well as the acclaimed novels *Le Mariage* and *L'Affaire.* She currently divides her time between Paris and San Francisco.

This book is set in Garamond 3, designed by
Morris Fuller Benton and Thomas Maitland
Cleland in the 1930s and released digitally
by Adobe.

Printed by R. R. Donnelley and Sons on
Gladfelter 60-pound Thor Offset smooth
white antique paper.

Cover printed by Moore Langen Printing.
Color separation by Quad Graphics.